AF479243

A Bibliography of Books of the Short Story

A Bibliography of Books of the Short Story

by

David Powell

The Whitston Publishing Company
Troy, New York
1978

To Maria,

whose work this also is

BIBLIOGRAPHY OF BOOKS OF THE
SHORT STORY

This bibliography is divided into these sections: I. Short-Story Collections, by Individual Authors.   II A. Cross-index, Short-Story Authors and Their Critics.   II B. Critics of Short-Story Authors.   III. Collections and Anthologies of the Short Story, More Than One Author.   IV. Mixed-Genre Anthologies Containing the Short Story.   V. History, Theory, and Criticism of the Short Story.

Other sources—indices, bibliographies, and periodicals—which the reader may consult are the following:

INDICES:

Chicorel, Marietta, ed. *Chicorel Index to Short Stories in Anthologies and Collections.* Chicorel Library, 1974.

Cook, Dorothy Elizabeth and Isabel S. Monro, compilers. *Short Story Index: an Index to 60,000 Stories in 4,320 Collections.* New York, H. W. Wilson, 1953.

—. Supplement 1950-1954, compiled by Dorothy E. Cook and Estelle A. Fidell. New York, H. W. Wilson, 1956.

—. Supplement 1955-1958, compiled by Estelle A. Fidell and Esther V. Flory. New York, H. W. Wilson, 1960.

—. Supplement 1959-1963, compiled by Estelle A. Fidell. New York, H. W. Wilson, 1965.

Hannigan, Francis J., compiler. *Standard Index of Short Stories, 1900-1914.* New York, The Library Reference Series, 1972 reprint of 1918 Gregg edition.

Wren, Sheila, ed. *Short Story Index Compiled from the*

Canadian Periodical Index, 1938-1947.   Canadian Library Association, 1967.

BIBLIOGRAPHIES:
Thurston, Jarvis, and others. *Short Fiction Criticism.* Denver, Alan Swallow Press, 1960.

Walker, Warren S. *Twentieth-Century Short Story Explication.*   Hamden, Connecticut, The Shoe String Press, 1967, with supplements from 1968.

PERIODICALS:
The principal periodicals on the short story are *Modern Fiction Studies,* Purdue University, and *Studies in Short Fiction,* Newberry College, Newberry, South Carolina. *Studies in Short Fiction,* Winter 1970 and supplemented Spring 1971, has a lengthy cross-referenced index of short fiction anthologies and author-title listing, compiled by Landon C. Burns.   Charles E. May's "The Short Story in the College Classroom: A Survey of Texts Published in the Sixties" appears in the January 1972 issue of *College English.   The Explicator, Nineteenth-Century Fiction,* and *Twentieth-Century Literature* occasionally provide useful commentaries on short fiction, and, as well as the above-named periodicals, include bibliographical items on the subject.

A Bibliography of Books of the Short Story

I. SHORT-STORY COLLECTIONS,
BY INDIVIDUAL AUTHORS

Ade, George. *Bang! Bang!* New York: J. H. Sears and Company, Inc., 1928. 147 pages.

—. *Fables in Slang.* New York: Grosset and Dunlap, 1899. 276 pages.

Agee, James. *The Collected Prose of James Agee,* ed. and with memoir by Robert Fitzgerald. Boston: Houghton Mifflin, 1968. 243 pages.

Aichinger, Ilse. *The Bound Man, and Other Stories,* tr. Eric Mosbacher. New York: Noonday Press, 1956. 100 pages.

Aiken, Conrad. *The Collected Stories of Conrad Aiken,* preface by Mark Schorer. Cleveland: World Publishing Company, 1960. 566 pages.

Aleichem, Sholom (*pseudonym* of Shalom Rabinowitz). *Selected Stories of Sholom Aleichem,* with introduction by Alfred Kazin. New York: Modern Liberary, 1956. 432 pages.

—. *Stories and Satires by Sholom Aleichem,* tr. Curt Leviant. New York: T. Yoseloff, 1959. 381 pages.

Algren, Nelson. *The Last Carousel.* New York: Putnam, 1973. 435 pages.

—. *The Neon Wilderness.* New York: Hill and Wang, 1960. 286 pages.

Anderson, Sherwood. *Death in the Woods, and Other Stories.* New York: Liveright, Inc., 1933. 298 pages.

Anderson, Sherwood. *Horses and Men.* London: Jonathan Cape Ltd., 1927. 220 pages.

—. *The Portable Sherwood Anderson,* ed. Horace Gregory. New York: Viking, 1949. 497 pages.

—. *The Sherwood Anderson Reader,* ed. Paul Rosenfeld. Boston: Houghton Mifflin, 1947. 850 pages.

—. *Sherwood Anderson: Short Stories,* ed. and with introduction by Maxwell Geismar. Hill and Wang, 1962. 289 pages.

—. *Sherwood Anderson's Notebook.* New York: Boni and Liveright, 1926. 280 pages.

—. *Story-Teller's Story.* Garden City, New York: Garden City Publishing Company, 1924. 442 pages.

—. *The Triumph of the Egg.* New York: B. W. Huebsch, 1921. 269 pages.

—. *Winesburg, Ohio,* introduction by Ernest Boyd. New York: Modern Library, 1919. 303 pages.

—. *Winesburg, Ohio: Text and Criticism,* ed. John H. Ferres. New York: Viking, 1966. 511 pages.

Aymé, Marcel. *Across Paris, and Other Stories,* tr. Norman Denny. New York: Harper, 1947. 254 pages.

—. *The Proverb, and Other Stories,* tr. Norman Denny. New York: Atheneum, 1961. 287 pages.

Babel, Isaac. *The Collected Stories,* ed. and tr. Walter Morison, with an introduction by Lionel Trilling. New York: Criterion Books, 1955. 381 pages.

—. *Lyubka, the Cossack, and Other Stories,* tr. Andrew MacAndrew. New York: New American Library, 1963. 285 pages.

—. *You Must Know Everything: Stories 1915-1937,* tr. Max Hayward; ed. and with notes by Nathalie Babel. New York:

Farrar, Straus and Giroux, 1969. 283 pages.

Baldwin, James. *Going to Meet the Man.* New York: Dial Press, 1965. 249 pages.

—. *No Name in the Street.* New York: Dial Press, 1972. 197 pages.

Balzac, Honoré de. *Short Stories.* New York: Marvin Press, 1931. 252 pages.

—. *Stories from Balzac,* ed. with notes and vocabulary by Douglas Labaree Buffum. New York: Henry Holt, 1917. 469 pages.

Barth, John. *Lost in the Funhouse.* Garden City, New York: Doubleday, 1968. 201 pages.

Barthelme, Donald. *City Life.* New York: Farrar, Straus and Giroux, 1970. 168 pages.

—. *Sadness.* New York: Farrar, Straus and Giroux, 1972. 183 pages.

Bates, H. E. *The Best of H. E. Bates,* with a preface by Henry Miller. Boston: Little, Brown, 1963. 454 pages.

—. *A Breath of Fresh Air.* Boston: Little, Brown, 1959. 209 pages.

—. *The Daffodil Sky.* Boston: Little, Brown, 1956. 256 pages.

—. *The Darling Buds of May.* Boston: Little, Brown, 1958 219 pages.

—. *The Day of the Tortoise.* London: Michael Joseph, 1961. 93 pages.

—. *Day's End and Other Stories.* New York: Viking, 1928. 286 pages.

—. *The Watercress Girl and Other Stories.* Boston: Little, Brown, 1959. 222 pages.

Bates, H. E. *Woman Who Had Imagination, and Other Stories.* Freeport, New York: Books for Libraries, reprint (1969) of 1934 edition. 288 pages.

Beckett, Samuel. *First Love, and Other Stories.* New York: Grove Press, 1974. 87 pages.

—. *More Pricks Than Kicks.* New York: Grove Press, 1970 191 pages.

—. *Stories and Texts for Nothing.* New York: Grove Press, 1967. 140 pages.

Bellow, Saul. *Mosby's Memoirs and Other Stories.* New York: Viking, 1968. 184 pages.

—. *The Portable Saul Bellow,* with critical introduction by Gabriel Josipovici. New York: Viking, 1974.

Bemelmans, Ludwig. *The World of Bemelmans.* New York: Viking, 1955. 503 pages.

Benét, Stephen Vincent. *The Devil and Daniel Webster.* New York: Holt, Rinehart, and Winston, 1965. 61 pages.

—. *The Last Circle: Stories and Poems.* New York: Farrar, Straus and Company, 1946. 309 pages.

—. *Selected Works of Stephen Vincent Benét.* New York: Farrar, Straus and Rinehart, Inc., 1942. 2 vols.

—. *Selected Works of Stephen Vincent Benét.* New York: Holt, Rinehart and Winston, 1955 and 1963. 2 vols.

—. *Thirteen O'Clock: Stories of Several Worlds.* New York: Toronto, Farrar and Rinehart, Inc., 1937. 305 pages.

Bennett, Arnold. *Elsie and the Child, and Other Stories.* New York: George H. Doran, 1924. 344 pages.

—. *The Matador of the Five Towns, and Other Stories.* New York: George H. Doran, 1912. 420 pages.

Bennett, Arnold. *The Woman Who Stole Everything, and Other Stories.* New York: George H. Doran, 1927. 350 pages.

Bierce, Ambrose. *Can Such Things Be?* New York: A. C. Boni, 1909. 427 pages.

—. *The Collected Works of Ambrose Bierce,* 12 vols. Staten Island, New York: Gordian Press, 1909-1912.

—. *The Collected Writings of Ambrose Bierce,* ed. and with introduction by Clifton Fadiman. New York: The Citadel Press, 1946. 810 pages.

—. *The Complete Short Stories of Ambrose Bierce,* ed. Ernest J. Hopkins. Garden City, New York: Doubleday, 1970. 496 pages.

—. *Ghost and Horror Stories,* ed. E. F. Bleiler. New York: Dover Publications, 1964. 199 pages.

—. *In the Midst of Life.* London: Nash and Grayson, 1923. 244 pages.

—. *Tales of Soldiers and Civilians.* New York: The Heritage Press, 1943. 220 pages.

Böll, Heinrich. *Children Are Civilians Too,* tr. Leila Vennewitz. New York: McGraw-Hill, 1970. 189 pages.

—. *Eighteen Stories,* tr. Leila Vennewitz. New York: McGraw-Hill, 1966. 243 pages.

—. *Traveler, If You Come to Spa.* München: M. Hueber Verlag, 1950. 119 pages.

Borges, Jorge Luis. *The Aleph and Other Stories, 1933-1969.* New York: E. P. Dutton, 1970. 286 pages.

—. *Ficciónes,* ed. and with introduction by Anthony Kerrigan. New York: Grove Press, 1962. 174 pages.

—. *Labyrinths, Selected Stories and Other Writings,* ed. Donald A. Yates and James E. Irby, with preface by André Maurois.

New York: New Directions, 1962. 248 pages.

Borges, Jorge Luis. *Personal Anthology,* ed. and with foreword by Anthony Kerrigan. New York: Grove Press, 1967. 210 pages.

Bowen, Elizabeth. *Ann Lee's, and Other Stories.* Freeport, New York: Books for Libraries Press, reprint (1969) of 1926 edition. 288 pages.

—. *The Cat Jumps, and Other Stories.* London: Jonathan Cape, 1949. 191 pages.

—. *The Demon Lover, and Other Stories.* London: Jonathan Cape, 1945. 189 pages.

—. *Ivy Gripped the Steps, and Other Stories.* New York: A. A. Knopf, 1946. 233 pages.

—. *Joining Charles, and Other Stories.* London: Jonathan Cape, c1929, 1952. 205 pages.

—. *Look at All Those Roses.* London: Jonathan Cape, 1951. 222 pages.

—. *Stories by Elizabeth Bowen.* New York: Vintage Books, 1959. 305 pages.

Boyle, Kay. *Thirty Stories.* New York: Simon and Schuster, 1946. 362 pages.

—. *Wedding Day and Other Stories.* Freeport, New York: Books for Libraries Press, reprint (1970) of 1929 edition. 122 pages.

Bradbury, Ray. *The Golden Apples of the Sun.* Westport, Connecticut: Greenwood Press, reprint (1970) of 1953 Doubleday edition. 250 pages.

Bunin, Ivan. *The Gentleman from San Francisco, and Other Stories.* New York: T. Seltzer, 1923. 135 pages.

Cable, George Washington. *Old Creole Days.* New York: Scribner's, 1897. 234 pages.

Cable, George Washington. *Strange True Stories of Louisiana.* Freeport, New York: Books for Libraries Press, reprint (1970) of 1889 edition. 350 pages.

—. *Strong Hearts.* Freeport, New York: Books for Libraries Press, reprint (1970) of 1899 edition. 214 pages.

Caldwell, Erskine. *The Courting of Susie Brown and Other Stories.* New York: Dell, Sloan and Pearce, 1952. 202 pages.

—. *Jackpot: The Short Stories of Erskine Caldwell.* New York: Duell, Sloan and Pearce, 1940. 756 pages.

—. *Kneel to the Rising Sun.* New York: Viking, 1935. 246 pages.

—. *We Are the Living.* New York: Viking, 1933. 264 pages.

Calisher, Hortense. *In the Absence of Angels.* Boston, Little, Brown 1951. 243 pages.

Campbell, William Edward March. *See* William March.

Camus, Albert. *Exile and the Kingdom.* New York: Random House, 1958. 213 pages.

Canfield, Dorothy. *A Harvest of Stories.* New York: Harcourt, Brace, 1956. 352 pages.

Capote, Truman. *The Grass Harp and A Tree of Night and Other Stories.* New York: New American Library, 1956. 216 pages.

—. *A Tree of Night and Other Stories.* New York: Random House, 1945. 137 pages.

Cary, Joyce. *Spring Song, and Other Stories.* New York: Harper, 1960. 285 pages.

Cather, Willa. *Collected Short Fiction, 1892-1912,* ed. Virginia

Faulkner; introduction by Mildred R. Bennett. Lincoln, University of Nebraska Press, 1965. 594 pages.

Cather, Willa. *Early Stories*, ed. Mildred R. Bennett. New York: Dodd, Mead, 1957. 275 pages.

—. *Obscure Destinies.* New York: A. A. Knopf, 1932. 229 pages.

—. *The Old Beauty, and Others.* New York: A. A. Knopf, 1948. 166 pages.

—. *The Troll Garden.* New York: New American Library, 1961. 152 pages.

—. *Uncle Valentine, and Other Stories*, ed. and with introduction by Bernice Slote. Lincoln, University of Nebraska Press, 1973. 183 pages.

—. *Youth and the Bright Medusa.* New York: A. A. Knopf, 1925. 303 pages.

Cheever, John. *The Brigadier and the Golf Widow.* New York: Harper and Row, 1964. 275 pages.

—. *The Enormous Radio, and Other Stories.* New York: Funk and Wagnalls, 1953. 237 pages.

—. *The Housebreaker of Shady Hill, and Other Stories.* New York: Harper, 1958. 185 pages.

—. *Some People, Places, and Things That Will Not Appear in My Next Novel.* New York: Harper, 1961. 175 pages.

—. *The Way Some People Live, a Book of Stories.* New York: Random House, 1943. 256 pages.

Chekhov, Anton. *The Bishop, and Other Stories*, tr. Constance Garnett. New York: Macmillan, 1919. 302 pages.

—. *The Black Monk, and Other Stories*, tr. R. E. C. Long. Freeport, New York: Books of Libraries Press, reprint (1970) of 1903 edition.

Chekhov, Anton. *The Chorus Girl, and Other Stories,* tr. Constance Garnett. New York: Macmillan, 1920. 301 pages.

—. *The Cook's Wedding, and Other Stories,* tr. Constance Garnett. New York: Macmillan, 1922. 308 pages.

—. *The Darling, and Other Stories,* tr. Constance Garnett, with introduction by Edward Garnett. New York: Willey Book Company, 1916. 329 pages.

—. *The Duel, and Other Stories,* tr. Constance Garnett. New York: Macmillan, 1916. 323 pages.

—. *Grasshopper and Other Stories,* tr. and with introduction by A. E. Chamot. Philadelphia: David McKay Company, 1926. 283 pages.

—. *The Horse-Stealers, and Other Stories,* tr. Constance Garnett. New York: Macmillan, 1921. 312 pages.

—. *The Kiss, and Other Stories,* tr. R. E. C. Long. New York: Frederick A. Stokes Company, 1916. 317 pages.

—. *The Lady with the Dog, and Other Stories,* tr. Constance Garnett. New York: Macmillan, 1928. 300 pages.

—. *Late-Blooming Flowers, and Other Stories,* tr. I. C. Chertok and Jean Gardner. New York: McGraw-Hill, 1964. 252 pages.

—. *Love, and Other Stories,* tr. Constance Garnett. New York: Macmillan, 1923. 306 pages.

—. *My Life, and Other Stories,* tr. S. S. Koteliansky and Gilbert Cannan. London: C. W. Daniel, Ltd., 1920. 251 pages.

—. *Nine Humorous Tales,* tr. Isaac Goldberg and Henry T. Schnittkind. Freeport, New York: Books for Libraries Press, reprint (1970) of 1918 edition. 60 pages.

—. *The Oxford Chekhov,* tr. and ed. Ronald Hingley. London: New York: Oxford University Press, 1964. 8 vols.

Chekhov, Anton. *The Party, and Other Stories*, tr. Constance Garnett. New York: Macmillan, 1917. 340 pages.

—. *Plays and Stories.* London: J. M. Dent and Sons, Ltd., 1937. 360 pages.

—. *The Portable Chekhov*, ed. Avrahm Yarmolinsky. New York: Viking, 1968. 634 pages.

—. *Rothschild's Fiddle, and Other Stories.* Freeport, New York: Books for Libraries Press, reprint (1970) of 1917 edition. 252 pages.

—. *Russian Silhouettes: More Stories of Russian Life*, tr. Marian Fell. New York: Scribner's, 1915. 318 pages.

—. *St. Peter's Day, and Other Tales*, tr., with introduction, by Frances H. Jones. New York: Capricorn, 1959. 191 pages.

—. *The Schoolmaster, and Other Stories*, tr. Constance Garnett. New York: Macmillan, 1921. 302 pages.

—. *Select Tales of Tchehov*, tr. Constance Garnett. London: Chatto and Windus, 1949. 594 pages.

—. *Selected Stories*, tr. Jessie Coulson. London; New York: Oxford University Press, 1963. 365 pages.

—. *Seven Short Stories*, tr. and introduction by Ronald Hingley. London; New York: Oxford University Press, 1974. 242 pages.

—. *The Short Stories of Anton Chekhov*, ed. and with introduction by Robert N. Linscott. New York: Modern Library, 1959. 448 pages.

—. *The Sinner from Toledo, and Other Stories*, tr. Arnold Hinchliffe. Rutherford, New Jersey, Fairleigh Dickinson University Press, 1972. 168 pages.

—. *The Steppe, and Other Stories*, tr. Adeline Lister Kaye. Freeport, New York: Books for Libraries Press, reprint (1970) of 1915 edition. 296 pages.

Chekhov, Anton. *Unknown Chekhov: Stories and Other Writings Hitherto Untranslated*, tr. and with introduction by Avrahm Yarmolinsky. New York: Noonday Press, 1954. 316 pages.

Chesterton, G. K. *The Father Brown Omnibus.* New York: Dodd, Mead, 1951. 993 pages.

—. *The Innocence of Father Brown.* New York: Macaulay, 1911. 334 pages.

—. *The Man Who Was Chesterton: The Best Essays, Stories, Poems and Other Writings of G. K. Chesterton,* compiled and edited by Raymond T. Bond. New York: Dodd, Mead and Company, 1937. 801 pages.

—. *Stories, Essays, and Poems,* introduction by Maisie Ward. London: Dent, 1935. 344 pages.

—. *Tales of the Long Bow.* London; New York: Cassell and Company, Ltd., 1925. 309 pages.

Chopin, Kate. *Awakening and Other Stories,* ed. Lewis Leary. New York: Holt, Rinehart and Winston, 1970. 341 pages.

—. *Bayou Folk.* Boston and New York: Houghton Mifflin and Company, 1894. 313 pages.

—. *The Complete Works of Kate Chopin,* ed. and with introduction by Per Seyersted. Baton Rouge, Louisiana: Louisiana State University Press, 1969. 2 vols.

—. *A Night in Acadie.* New York: Garrett Press, 1968, reprint of 1897 edition. 416 pages.

Clark, Walter Van Tilburg. *The Watchful Gods, and Other Stories.* New York: Random House, 1950. 306 pages.

Collier, John. *Fancies and Goodnights.* Garden City, New York: Doubleday, 1956. 364 pages.

—. *His Monkey Wife.* Garden City, New York: Doubleday, 1957. 259 pages.

Collier, John. *The John Collier Reader.* New York: A. A. Knopf, 1972. 571 pages.

Connell, Evan S. *Anatomy Lesson and Other Stories.* Freeport, New York: Books for Libraries Press, 1970 reprint of 1957 edition.

Connell, Richard. *Apes and Angels.* Freeport, New York: Books for Libraries Press, 1970 reprint of 1924 edition. 312 pages.

—. *The Most Dangerous Game.* Brandt and Brandt, 1924.

Conrad, Joseph. *Complete Works.* New York: Doubleday, Page, 1925. 26 vols.

—. *A Conrad Argosy.* Garden City, New York: Doubleday, Doran and Company, 1942. 713 pages.

—. *The Portable Conrad,* ed. Morton D. Zabel and Frederick R. Karl. New York: Viking, 1947. 762 pages.

—. *Selected Stories.* Garden City, New York: Doubleday, Doran, 1903. 2 vols. in 1.

—. *The Shorter Tales of Joseph Conrad.* Freeport, New York: Books for Libraries Press, 1970 reprint of 1924 edition. 452 pages.

—. *Tales of the East and West,* ed. and with introduction by Morton Dauwen Zabel. Garden City, New York: Hanover House, 1958. 544 pages.

—. *Tales of Land and Sea.* Garden City, New York: Hanover House, 1953. 695 pages.

—. *The Works of Joseph Conrad.* London: Gresham Publishing Company, 1925-1927. 21 vols.

Coppard, A. E. *Adam and Eve and Pinch Me.* Freeport, New York: Books for Libraries Press, 1970 reprint of 1922 edition. 331 pages.

Coppard, A. E. *The Black Dog and Other Stories.* Freeport, New York: Books for Libraries Press, 1970 reprint of 1923 edition. 294 pages.

—. *The Collected Tales of A. E. Coppard.* New York: A. A. Knopf, 1948. 532 pages.

—. *Fishmonger's Fiddle.* Freeport, New York: Books for Libraries Press, 1970 reprint of 1925 edition. 320 pages.

—. *Ninepenny Flute: Twenty-One Tales.* Freeport, New York: Books for Libraries Press, 1970 reprint of 1937 edition. 305 pages.

—. *Nixey's Harlequin.* London: Jonathan Cape, Ltd., 1931. 296 pages.

—. *Polly Oliver: Tales.* Freeport, New York: Books for Libraries Press, 1970 reprint of 1935 edition. 320 pages.

Cortazar, Julio. *Blow-Up and Other Stories,* tr. Paul Blackburn. New York: Collier Books, 1967. 248 pages.

—. *End of the Game, and Other Stories,* tr. Paul Blackburn. New York: Pantheon, 1967. 277 pages.

Crane, Stephen. *The Last Words.* London: Digby, Long and Company, 1902. 320 pages.

—. *The Little Regiment, and Other Episodes of the American Civil War.* Freeport, New York: Books for Libraries Press, 1971 reprint of 1896 edition. 196 pages.

—. *Men, Women and Boats,* ed. and with introduction by Vincent Starrett. Freeport, New York: Books for Libraries Press, 1970 reprint of 1921 edition. 245 pages.

—. *The Open Boat, and Other Tales of Adventure.* New York: Doubleday and McClure Company, 1898. 336 pages.

—. *The Portable Stephen Crane,* ed. Joseph Katz. New York: Viking, 1969. 550 pages.

Crane, Stephen. *The Red Badge of Courage, and Other Stories.* New York: Dodd, Mead, 1957. 409 pages.

—. *Stephen Crane: An Omnibus,* ed. Robert Wooster Stallman. New York: A. A. Knopf, 1952. 703 pages.

—. *The Stephen Crane Reader,* ed. Robert Wooster Stallman. Glenview, Illinois: Scott, Foresman, 1972. 604 pages.

—. *Stories and Tales,* ed. Robert Wooster Stallman. New York: Vintage Books, 1955. 350 pages.

—. *The Sullivan County Sketches of Stephen Crane.* Syracuse, New York: Syracuse University Press, 1949. 85 pages.

—. *Sullivan County Tales and Sketches.* Ames, Iowa: Iowa State University Press, 1968. 151 pages.

—. *Whilomville Stories.* New York: Garrett Press, 1969, reprint of the 1900 edition. 198 pages.

—. *The Works of Stephen Crane,* 12 vols. New York: A. A. Knopf, 1925-1927.

—. *Wounds in the Rain.* New York: Frederick A. Stokes, 1900. 347 pages.

Dahl, Ronald. *Kiss Kiss.* New York: Knopf, 1959. 308 pages.

—. *Someone Like You.* New York: Knopf, 1953. 359 pages.

Daudet, Alphonse. *La Belle-Nivernaise, and Other Stories.* Freeport, New York: Books for Libraries Press, 1970 reprint of 1895 edition. 221 pages.

—. *Letters from My Mill and Letters to an Absent One.* New York: Dodd, Mead and Company, 1893. 263 pages.

—. *Monday Tales.* Freeport, New York: Books for Libraries Press, 1970 reprint of 1900 edition. 326 pages.

—. *Selected Short Stories of Alphonse Daudet.* New York: Barnes, 1974.

Defoe, Daniel. *The Novels and Selected Writings of Daniel Defoe*, 14 vols. Totowa, New Jersey: Rowman and Littlefield, 1974 reprint of 1923 edition.

De Quincey, Thomas. *The Collected Writings of Thomas De Quincey*, 14 vols., ed. David Masson. Edinburgh: A. and C. Black, 1889-1890.

Dinesen, Isak. *Last Tales.* New York: Random House, 1957. 341 pages.

—. *Seven Gothic Tales.* New York: Modern Library, 1934. 420 pages.

—. *Winter's Tales.* New York: Random House, 1942. 313 pages.

Dostoyevsky, Fyodor. *Best Short Stories,* tr. David Magarshack. New York: Modern Library, 1955. 322 pages.

—. *The Diary of a Writer,* tr. Boris Brasol, 2 vols. New York: Scribner's, 1949. 1097 pages.

—. *An Honest Thief and Other Stories,* tr. Constance Garnett. New York: Macmillan, 1919. 325 pages.

—. *The Short Stories of Dostoyevsky,* ed. and with introduction by William Phillips. New York: Dial Press, 1946. 614 pages.

Dreiser, Theodore. *The Best Short Stories of Theodore Dreiser,* ed. and with introduction by Howard Fast. Cleveland and New York: The World Publishing Company, 1947. 349 pages.

Dunbar, Paul Laurence. *Folks from Dixie.* New York: Negro University Press, 1969 reprint of 1898 edition. 263 pages.

—. *The Heart of Happy Hollow.* New York: Dodd, Mead and Company, 1904. 309 pages.

—. *The Life and Works of Paul Laurence Dunbar,* collected and with biography of Lida Keck Wiggins. New York: Kraus reprint of 1907 edition. 430 pages.

Dunbar, Paul Laurence. *The Paul Laurence Dunbar Reader.* New York: Dodd, Mead, 1975. 477 pages.

—. *Strength of Gideon, and Other Stories.* New York: Arno Press, 1969 reprint of 1900 publication. 362 pages.

Dunne, Finley Peter. *Mr. Dooley at His Best,* ed. Elmer Ellis. Hamden, Connecticut: Anchor Books, 1949. 291 pages.

Elkin, Stanley. *Criers and Kibitzers, Kibitzers and Criers: Nine Stories.* New York: Random House, 1965. 272 pages.

Ellison, Ralph. *Invisible Man.* New York: Random House, 1952. 439 pages.

Farrell, James T. *An Omnibus of Short Stories.* New York: Vanguard Press, 1956. 313 pages.

—. *The Short Stories of James T. Farrell,* with preface by Farrell and introduction by Robert Morss Lovett. New York: Vanguard Press, 1934. 534 pages.

Faulkner, William. *The Best of Faulkner.* London: Reprint Society, 1955. 494 pages.

—. *Big Woods: The Hunting Stories of William Faulkner.* New York: Random House, 1955. 198 pages.

—. *Collected Stories.* New York: Random House, 1950. 900 pages.

—. *Faulkner in the University,* ed. Frederick L. Gwynn and Joseph L. Blotner. Charlottesville, Virginia: University of Virginia Press, 1959. 294 pages.

—. *The Faulkner Reader.* New York: Random House, 1954. 682 pages.

—. *Go Down, Moses and Other Stories.* New York: Random House, 1942. 383 pages.

Faulkner, William. *The Portable Faulkner,* ed. Malcolm Cowley. New York: Viking, 1946. 756 pages.

—. *Selected Short Stories.* New York: Modern Library, 1961. 306 pages.

Fitzgerald, F. Scott. *All the Sad Young Men.* New York: Scribner's, 1926. 267 pages.

—. *The Apprentice Fiction of F. Scott Fitzgerald,* ed. John Kuehl. New Brunswick, New Jersey: Rutgers University Press, 1965. 184 pages.

—. *Babylon Revisited and Other Stories.* New York: Scribner's, 1960. 253 pages.

—. *The Basil and Josephine Stories.* New York: Scribner's, 1973. 287 pages.

—. *The Bodley Head Scott Fitzgerald.* London: Bodley Head, 4 vols., 1958-1961.

—. *The Fitzgerald Reader,* ed. Arthur Mizener. New York: Scribner's, 1963. 509 pages.

—. *Flappers and Philosophers.* New York: Scribner's, 1959. 189 pages.

—. *The Pat Hobby Stories.* New York: Scribner's, 1962. 159 pages.

—. *The Portable F. Scott Fitzgerald.* New York: Viking, 1945. 835 pages.

—. *Six Tales of the Jazz Age, and Other Stories.* New York: Scribner's, 1960. 192 pages.

—. *The Stories of F. Scott Fitzgerald,* ed. and with introduction by Malcolm Cowley. New York: Scribner's, 1951. 473 pages.

—. *Tales of the Jazz Age.* New York: Scribner's, 1922. 317 pages.

Fitzgerald, F. Scott. *Taps at Reveille.* New York: Scribner's, 1960. 341 pages.

Flandrau, Charles Macomb. *Harvard Episodes.* Freeport, New York: Books for Libraries Press, 1969 reprint of 1897 edition. 339 pages.

Flaubert, Gustave. *Three Tales,* tr. Robert Baldick. Harmondsworth, Middlesex, England: Penguin Books, Inc., 1961. 124 pages.

Forster, E. M. *Abinger Harvest.* New York: Harcourt, Brace, 1936. 363 pages.

—. *The Celestial Omnibus, and Other Stories.* London: Sidgwick and Jackson, Ltd., 1911. 163 pages.

—. *The Collected Tales of E. M. Forster.* New York: A. A. Knopf, 1947. 308 pages.

—. *The Eternal Moment, and Other Stories.* New York: Grosset and Dunlap, 1956. 245 pages.

—. *The Life to Come, and Other Short Stories.* New York: W. W. Norton, 1972. 240 pages.

France, Anatole. *Crainquebille.* New York: Heritage Press, 1949. 69 pages.

—. *Crainquebille,* tr. Winifred Stephens. Freeport, New York: Books for Libraries Press, 1970 reprint of 1922 edition. 236 pages.

—. *Golden Tales of Anatole France.* New York: Dodd, Mead and Company, 1927. 352 pages.

—. *Great Short Stories of Anatole France.* New York: Henry Holt and Company, 1936. 188 pages.

—. *The Merrie Tales of Jacques Tournebroche, and Child Life in Town and Country,* tr. Alfred Allinson. Freeport, New York: Books for Libraries Press, 1970 reprint of 1909 edition. 230 pages.

France, Anatole. *Mother of Pearl,* tr. Frederic Chapman. London: John Lane; New York: Dodd, Mead, 1924.   337 pages.

—. *Seven Wives of Bluebeard.*   Freeport, New York: Books for Libraries, 1971 reprint of 1923 edition. 231 pages.

Freeman, Mary E. Wilkins. *The Copy-Cat, and Other Stories.* New York and Harper and Brothers, 1914. 350 pages.

—. *The Givers.*   New York: Garrett Press, 1969.   295 pages.

—. *The Humble Romance, and Other Stories.*   New York: Garrett Press, 1969 reprint of 1887 edition.   436 pages.

—. *The Love of Parson Lord, and Other Stories.*   Freeport, New York: Books for Libraries Press, 1969 reprint of 1900 edition.   232 pages.

—. *A New England Nun, and Other Stories.*   New York: Harper and Brothers, 1891.   468 pages.

—. *The People of Our Neighborhood.*   Freeport, New York: Books for Libraries, 1970 reprint of 1898 edition.   161 pages.

—. *Pot of Gold, and Other Stories.*   Freeport, New York: Books for Libraries, 1970 reprint of 1892 edition.   324 pages.

—. *Silence, and Other Stories.*   Freeport, New York: Books for Libraries Press, 1969 reprint of 1898 edition.   279 pages.

—. *Six Trees: Short Stories.*   Freeport, New York: Books for Libraries Press, 1969 reprint of 1903 edition.   206 pages.

—. *Understudies: Short Stories.*   Freeport, New York: Books for Libraries Press, 1969 reprint of 1901 edition.   229 pages.

—. *The Wind in the Rose-Bush and Other Stories of the Supernatural.*   New York: Garrett Press, 1969 reprint of 1903 edition.   237 pages.

Freeman, Mary E. Wilkins. *Young Lucretius, and Other Stories.* Freeport, New York: Books for Libraries Press, 1970 reprint of 1892 edition. 258 pages.

Galsworthy, John. *Galsworthy Reader*, ed. Anthony West. New York: Scribner's, 1967. 702 pages.

Garland, Hamlin. *Main-Travelled Roads.* Cambridge, Massachusetts and Chicago: Stone and Kimball, 1893. 251 pages.

—. *Prairie Folks.* New York: Garrett Press, 1969 reprint of 1899 edition. 284 pages.

—. *Wayside Courtships.* Freeport, New York: Books for Libraries Press, 1969 reprint of 1897 edition. 281 pages.

Gogol, Nikolai. *Collected Tales and Plays.* New York: Pantheon Books, 1964. 768 pages.

—. *Diary of a Madman and Other Stories*, tr. Ronald Wilks. Harmondsworth, Middlesex, England: Penguin Books, Inc., 1975. 188 pages.

—. *The Overcoat, and Other Stories.* New York: A. A. Knopf, 1923. 262 pages.

—. *Taras Bulba, and Other Tales.* London: J. M. Dent and Sons, Ltd.; New York: E. P. Dutton and Company, 1918. 311 pages.

Gordimer, Nadine. *Not for Publication, and Other Stories.* New York: Viking, 1965. 248 pages.

—. *The Soft Voice of the Serpent, and Other Stories.* New York: Simon and Schuster, 1952. 244 pages.

Gordon, Caroline. *Aleck Maury Sportsman.* New York: Scribner's, 1934. 287 pages.

—. *The Forest of the South.* New York: Scribner's, 1945. 245 pages.

—. *Old Red, and Other Stories.* New York: Scribner's, 1963.

256 pages.

Gorky, Maxim. *Best Short Stories.* New York: Grayson Publishing Corporation, 1947. 403 pages.

—. *A Book of Short Stories,* ed. Avrahm Yarmolinsky and Moura Budberg. New York: Farrar, Straus, and Giroux, reprint of 1939 edition. 358 pages.

—. *Creatures That Once Were Men.* New York: Boni and Liveright, 1918. 249 pages.

Greene, Graham. *Collected Stories.* New York: Viking, 1972. 561 pages.

—. *Nineteen Stories.* London: W. Heinemann, 1947. 231 pages.

—. *The Portable Graham Greene,* ed. Philip Stratford. New York: Viking, 1973. 610 pages.

—. *Twenty-One Stories.* London: Heinemann, 1958. 239 pages.

Hardy, Thomas. *A Changed Man, The Waiting Supper, and Other Tales.* London: Macmillan, 1951. 398 pages.

—. *Great Short Works of Thomas Hardy,* ed. Samuel Hynes. New York: Harper-Row, 1967. 387 pages.

—. *Life's Little Ironies.* New York: Harper and Brothers, 1894. 268 pages.

—. *Selected Short Stories of Thomas Hardy.* Allentown, Pennsylvania: Story Classics, 1948. 186 pages.

—. *Wessex Tales.* New York: Peter T. Collier, n.d. 347 pages.

—. *Works.* New York: Harper, 1905. 20 vols.

—. *Works.* London: Macmillan, 1919-1920. 37 vols.

Harris, Joel Chandler. *Balaam and His Master, and Other Sketches and Stories.* New York: McKinlay, Stone and Mackenzie, 1919. 293 pages.

Harris, Joel Chandler. *Free Joe, and Other Georgia Sketches.* Ridgewood, New Jersey: Gregg Press, 1967 reprint of 1887 edition. 236 pages.

—. *Mingo, and Other Sketches in Black and White.* New York: McKinlay, Stone and Mackenzie, 1912. 273 pages.

—. *Plantation Pageants.* Boston: Houghton Mifflin and Company, 1899. 247 pages.

—. *Tales of the Home Folks in Peace and War.* New York: MacKinlay, Stone and Mackenzie, 1898. 417 pages.

Harte, Bret. *The Best Short Stories of Bret Harte.* New York: Modern Library, 1947. 517 pages.

—. *The Luck of Roaring Camp and Other Sketches.* Boston: Houghton Mifflin and Company, 1898. 256 pages.

—. *Representative Selections.* New York: American Book Company, 1941. 416 pages.

—. *Stories in Light and Shadow.* New York: P. F. Collier and Son, 1889. 484 pages.

—. *Tales of Trail and Town.* Boston: Houghton Mifflin and Company, 1899. 348 pages.

—. *The Writings of Bret Harte.* New York: AMS Press, 1966. 20 vols.

Hawthorne, Nathaniel. *The Best Known Works of Nathaniel Hawthorne.* Garden City, New York: Halcyon House, 1941. 511 pages.

—. *Biographical Stories.* Boston: Houghton Mifflin and Company, 1883. 82 pages.

—. *The Complete Novels and Selected Tales of Nathaniel Hawthorne.* New York: Modern Library, 1937. 1223 pages.

—. *The Complete Works of Nathaniel Hawthorne.* London: Kegan Paul, Trench, 1883. 12 vols.

Hawthorne, Nathaniel. *Hawthorne's Short Stories,* ed. Newton Arvin. New York: A. A. Knopf, 1946. 422 pages.

—. *Mosses from an Old Manse.* Boston: Houghton Mifflin and Company, 1891. 559 pages.

—. *The Portable Hawthorne,* ed. Malcolm Cowley. New York: Viking, 1948. 634 pages.

—. *Representative Selections.* New York: American Book Company, 1934. 368 pages.

—. *Short Stories.* New York: Dodd, Mead, 1962. 422 pages.

—. *The Snow Image and Other Twice-Told Tales.* New York: Crowell and Company, 1899. 253 pages.

—. *Tales, Sketches, and Other Papers,* with a biographical sketch by George Parsons Lathrop. Boston: Houghton Mifflin and Company, 1887. 578 pages.

—. *Tales of the White Hills, and Sketches.* Boston: Houghton Mifflin and Company, 1894. 94 pages.

—. *Twice-Told Tales.* New York: F. M. Lupton Publishing Company, n.d. 288 pages.

—. *A Wonder Book.* Boston: Houghton Mifflin and Company, 1891. 637 pages.

Hemingway, Ernest. *The Fifth Column and the First Forty-Nine Stories.* New York: Scribner's, 1938.

—. *Hemingway Reader,* ed. Charles Poore. New York: Scribner's, 1953. 652 pages.

—. *In Our Time.* New York: Scribner's, 1953. 212 pages.

—. *Men at War,* ed. Ernest Hemingway. New York: Crown Publishers, 1942. 1072 pages.

—. *Men Without Women.* New York: Scribner's, 1927. 232 pages.

Hemingway, Ernest. *The Nick Adams Stories.* New York: Scribner's, 1972. 268 pages.

—. *Short Stories of Ernest Hemingway.* New York: Scribner's, 1953. 499 pages.

—. *The Snows of Kilimanjaro and Other Stories.* New York: Scribner's, 1953. 499 pages.

—. *Winner Take Nothing.* New York: Scribner's, 1933. 244 pages.

Henry, O. *The Best Short Stories of O. Henry.* New York: Modern Library, 1945. 338 pages.

—. *Cabbages and Kings.* New York: A. L. Burt Company, 1904. 312 pages.

—. *The Complete Works of O. Henry.* Garden City, New York: Doubleday, 1953. 1692 pages.

—. *The Four Million.* New York: A. L. Burt Company, 1906. 261 pages.

—. *The Gentle Grafter.* Garden City, New York: Doubleday, Page, 1908. 237 pages.

—. *Heart of the West.* Garden City, New York: Doubleday, Page, 1904. 313 pages.

—. *Options.* New York: Grosset and Dunlap, 1909. 324 pages.

—. *Roads and Destiny.* Garden City, New York: Doubleday, Page, 1909. 312 pages.

—. *Rolling Stones.* Garden City, New York: Doubleday, Page and Company, 1913. 292 pages.

—. *Sixes and Sevens.* Garden City, New York: Doubleday, Page, 1911. 283 pages.

—. *The Trimmed Lamp.* Garden City, New York: Doubleday, Page, 1907. 260 pages.

Henry, O. *The Voice of the City.* Garden City, New York: Doubleday, Page, 1908. 244 pages.

—. *Whirligigs.* Garden City, New York: Doubleday, Page, 1910. 314 pages.

Hoffmann, E. T. A. *Tales of E. T. A. Hoffmann,* ed. and tr. Leonard J. Kent and Elizabeth C. Knight. Chicago: University of Chicago Press, 1972. 279 pages.

Hofmannsthal, Hugo von. *Selected Writings,* ed. Michael Hamburger. 3 vols. Princeton, New Jersey: Princeton University Press, 1952-1963.

Howells, William Dean. *A Fearful Responsibility, and Other Stories.* Westport, Connecticut: Greenwood Press, reprint of 1881 edition. 255 pages.

Hughes, Langston. *An African Treasury.* New York: Crown Publishers, 1960. 207 pages.

—. *The Best Short Stories by Negro Writers.* Boston: Little, Brown, 1967. 508 pages.

—. *Something in Common, and Other Stories.* New York: Hill and Wang, 1960. 236 pages.

Huxley, Aldous. *Collected Short Stories.* New York: Bantam, 1960.

—. *Crome Yellow.* New York: George H. Doran and Company, 1922.

—. *Great Short Works of Aldous Huxley,* ed. Bernard Bergonzi. New York: Harper-Row, 1969. 483 pages.

—. *Mortal Coils.* New York: George H. Doran, 1922.

—. *The World of Aldous Huxley,* ed. and with introduction by Charles J. Rolo. New York: Harper, 1947.

Irving, Washington. *The Complete Tales of Washington Irving.* Garden City, New York: Doubleday, 1975. 798 pages.

Jackson, Shirley. *Come Along With Me,* ed. Stanley Edgar Hyman. New York: Viking, 1968. 243 pages.

—. *The Magic of Shirley Jackson,* ed. Stanley Edgar Hyman. New York: Farrar, Straus and Giroux, 1966. 753 pages.

Jacobs, William Wymark. *The Lady of the Barge and Other Stories.* New York: Dodd, Mead, 1902. 300 pages.

—. *Snug Harbour, Collected Stories by W. W. Jacobs.* New York: Scribner's, 1935. 681 pages.

James, Henry. *The Altar of the Dead and Other Tales.* New York: Scribner's, 1963. 541 pages.

—. *The American Novels and Stories of Henry James.* New York: A. A. Knopf, 1947. 993 pages.

—. *Americans and Europe: Selected Tales of Henry James,* ed. Napier Wilt and John Lucas. Boston: Houghton Mifflin, 1965. 441 pages.

—. *The Complete Tales of Henry James,* ed. Leon Edel, 12 vols. Philadelphia and London: Lippincott, 1962-1964.

—. *Eight Uncollected Tales.* New Brunswick, New Jersey: Rutgers University Press, 1950. 314 pages.

—. *The Ghostly Tales of Henry James.* New Brunswick, New Jersey: Rutgers University Press, 1948. 765 pages.

—. *Great Short Works of Henry James,* ed. Dean Flower. New York: Harper-Row, 1966. 490 pages.

—. *Novels and Tales of Henry James.* New York: Scribner's, 26 vols., 1961-1964.

—. *The Portable Henry James,* ed. Morton Dauwen Zabel. New York: Viking, 1956. 696 pages.

—. *Selected Fiction.* New York: Dutton, 1953. 609 pages.

—. *The Short Stories of Henry James,* ed. and with critical after-notes by Clifton Fadiman. New York: Random House, 1945. 644 pages.

James, Henry. *The Turn of the Screw, The Aspern Papers, and Other Stories.* London: Collins, 1956. 480 pages.

Jewett, Sarah Orne. *The Best Stories of Sarah Orne Jewett,* 2 vols., with preface by Willa Cather. Gloucester, Massachusetts, 1925. 2 vols. in 1.

—. *Country By-Ways.* Boston: Houghton Mifflin and Company, 1899. 249 pages.

—. *The Country of the Pointed Firs and Other Stories,* with preface by Willa Cather. New York: P. Smith, 1949. 2 vols. in 1.

Joyce, James. *Dubliners,* introduction by Padraic Colum. New York: Modern Library, 1954. 288 pages.

—. *Dubliners.* New York: B. W. Huebsch, Inc., 1925. 288 pages.

—. *Dubliners,* ed. Robert Scholes and Walton A. Litz. New York: Viking, 1969. 224 pages.

—. *The Essential James Joyce.* London: Jonathan Cape, 1948. 533 pages.

—. *The Portable James Joyce,* ed. Harry Levin. New York: Viking, 1947. 760 pages.

Kafka, Franz. *The Complete Stories.* New York: Schocken Books, 1971. 486 pages.

—. *Stories and Short Pieces.* New York: Schocken Books, 1948. 317 pages.

Kipling, Rudyard. *The Best of Kipling.* Garden City, New York: Doubleday, 1968. 669 pages.

—. *The Best Short Stories of Rudyard Kipling,* ed. and with introduction by Randall Jarrell. Garden City, New York:

Hanover House, 1961. 693 pages.

Kipling, Rudyard. *The Bombay Edition of the Works of Rudyard Kipling,* 26 vols. London: Macmillan, 1913.

—. *The Day's Work.* New York: Doubleday and McClure Company, 1898. 431 pages.

—. *Plain Tales from the Hills.* New York: Thomas Crowell, 1887. 317 pages.

—. *Soldiers Three.* New York: Burt, n.d. 366 pages.

—. *Wee Willie Winkie, and Other Stories.* Chicago: Rand McNally, n.d. 226 pages.

—. *Works.* New York: P. F. Collier and Sons, 1912, 10 vols.

La Farge, Oliver. *The Door in the Wall: Stories by Oliver La Farge.* Boston: Houghton Mifflin, 1965. 303 pages.

—. *A Pause in the Desert.* Boston: Houghton Mifflin, 1957. 235 pages.

Lagerkvist, Pär. *The Eternal Smile, and Other Stories.* New York: Hill and Wang, 1971. 206 pages.

Lardner, Ring. *The Collected Short Stories.* New York: Modern Library, 1941. 467 pages.

—. *Gullible's Travels, Etc.* Chicago: University of Chicago Press, 1965. 140 pages.

—. *The Portable Ring Lardner.* New York: Viking, 1946.

—. *The Ring Lardner Reader,* ed. Maxwell Geismar. New York: Scribner's, 1963.

—. *Round Up.* New York: Scribner's, 1929. 467 pages.

—. *Treat 'Em Rough.* Indianapolis: Bobbs-Merrill, 1918. 160 pages.

Lavin, Mary. *Collected Stories,* with introduction by V. S. Pritchett. Boston: Houghton Mifflin, 1971. 425 pages.

—. *Happiness and Other Stories.* London: Constable, 1969. 152 pages.

—. *In the Middle of the Fields, and Other Stories.* New York: Macmillan, 1969. 215 pages.

Lawrence, D. H. *The Complete Short Stories: D. H. Lawrence,* 3 vols. New York: Viking, 1961.

Lessing, Doris. *African Stories.* New York: Simon and Schuster, 1965. 636 pages.

—. *The Habit of Loving.* New York: Crowell, 1957. 311 pages.

—. *A Man and Two Women.* New York: Simon and Schuster, 1963. 316 pages.

—. *The Temptation of Jack Orkney and Other Stories.* New York: A. A. Knopf, 1972. 308 pages.

Lewis, Sinclair. *The Man Who Knew Coolidge.* New York: Harcourt, Brace, 1928. 275 pages.

—. *Selected Short Stories.* New York: Doubleday, Doran and Company, 1937. 426 pages.

London, Jack. *Best Short Stories of Jack London.* Garden City, New York: The Sun Dial Press, 1945. 311 pages.

—. *The Call of the Wild, and Other Stories.* New York: Dodd, Mean, 1960. 242 pages.

—. *The God of His Fathers and Other Stories.* New York: Mc-Clure, Phillips and Company, 1901. 299 pages.

—. *The House of Pride, and Other Tales of Hawaii.* New York: Grosset and Dunlap, 1912. 232 pages.

Lytle, Andrew. *A Novel, a Novella, and Four Stories.* New York: McDowell, Obolensky, 1958. 327 pages.

McCullers, Carson. *The Ballad of the Sad Café and Other Stories.* New York: Bantam Books, 1962, c1951. 152 pages.

—. *Mortgaged Heart.* Boston: Houghton Mifflin, 1971. 292 pages.

Malamud, Bernard. *Idiots First.* New York: Farrar, Straus and Giroux, 1963. 212 pages.

—. *The Magic Barrel.* New York: Farrar Straus and Cudahy, 1958. 214 pages.

—. *A Malamud Reader.* New York: Farrar, Straus and Giroux, 1967. 528 pages.

—. *Pictures of Fidelman.* New York: Farrar, Straus and Giroux, 1969. 208 pages.

Mann, Thomas. *Children and Fools,* tr. Herman George Scheffauer. New York: A. A. Knopf, 1928. 264 pages.

—. *Death in Venice,* tr. Kenneth Burke. New York: Bantam Books, 1925. 122 pages.

—. *Stories of Three Decades.* New York: Modern Library, 1961, c1936. 567 pages.

Mansfield, Katherine. *Bliss and Other Stories.* New York: A. A. Knopf, 1924. 277 pages.

—. *The Dove's Nest and Other Stories.* New York: A. A. Knopf, 1923. 242 pages.

—. *The Garden Party, and Other Stories.* New York: A. A. Knopf, 1922. 255 pages.

—. *Journal of Katherine Mansfield.* New York: A. A. Knopf, 1927. 255 pages.

—. *The Short Stories of Katherine Mansfield.* New York: A. A. Knopf, 1937. 688 pages.

March, William (*pseudonym* of William Edward March Campbell). *Trial Balance: The Collected Short Stories of William March.* Westport, Connecticut: Greenwood Press, reprint, 1971 of 1945 edition. 506 pages.

Maugham, W. Somerset. *Best Short Stories of Somerset Maugham.* New York: Modern Library, 1957. 489 pages.

—. *Complete Short Stories.* Garden City, New York: Doubleday, 1952. 2 vols.

—. *Cosmopolitans.* Garden City, New York: Doubleday, Doran, 1936. 272 pages.

—. *East and West: The Collected Short Stories of Somerset Maugham.* Garden City, New York: Doubleday, Doran and Company, Inc., 1934. 955 pages.

—. *The Maugham Reader.* Garden City, New York: Garden City Books, 1950. 1217 pages.

—. *Quartet.* Garden City, New York: Doubleday, 1949. 189 pages.

—. *Seventeen Lost Stories.* Garden City, New York: Doubleday, 1969. 273 pages.

Maupassant, Guy de. *The Best of Maupassant.* Emmaus, Pennsylvania: Story Classics, 1950. 246 pages.

—. *The Best Stories of Guy de Maupassant.* New York: Random House, 1945. 551 pages.

—. *The Complete Short Stories of de Maupassant.* New York: Halcyon House, 1947. 1011 pages.

—. *The Complete Short Stories of Guy de Maupassant.* New York: W. J. Black, 1903. 1003 pages.

—. *The Life Work of Henri René Guy de Maupassant.* London and New York: M. W. Dune, 1903, 17 vols.

—. *Mademoiselle Fifi, and Twelve Other Stories.* New York: Boni and Liveright, Inc., 1917. 251 pages.

Maupassant, Guy de. *The Novels and Tales of Guy de Maupassant.* London: A. A. Knopf, 1926. 13 vols.

—. *The Portable Maupassant.* New York: Viking, 1947. 756 pages.

—. *Selections from Guy de Maupassant.* Boston: Ginn, 1920. 166 pages.

—. *The Short Stories of Guy de Maupassant.* New York: Modern Library, 1932. 251 pages.

—. *Tales.* London: Curwer Press, 1963. 472 pages.

Melville, Herman. *The Apple-Tree Table and Other Stories.* Westport, Connecticut: Greenwood Press, reprint, 1971 of 1922 edition. 329 pages.

—. *Billy Budd, Benito Cereno, and The Enchanted Isles.* New York: Readers Club, 1942. 245 pages.

—. *Works.* New York: Russell and Russell, 1963. 16 vols.

Mérimée, Prosper. *Stories from Mérimée.* New York: Holt, 1947. 306 pages.

Michener, James A. *Tales of the South Pacific.* New York: Macmillan, 1947. 326 pages.

Moore, George. *The Collected Works of George Moore.* New York: Boni and Liveright, 1922-1924. 21 vols.

Moravia, Alberto. *Bitter Honeymoon, and Other Stories.* New York: Farrar, Straus, and Cudahy, 1956. 221 pages.

—. *The Fetish, and Other Stories.* New York: Farrar, Straus and Giroux, 1964. 285 pages.

—. *Roman Tales,* tr. Angus Davidson. New York: Farrar, Straus and Giroux, 1957. 229 pages.

—. *The Wayward Wife, and Other Stories.* New York: Farrar, Straus and Giroux, 1960. 221 pages.

Munro, H. H. ("Saki"). *Beasts and Super-Beasts.* New York: Viking, 1929. 240 pages.

—. *The Best of Saki,* selected and with an introduction by Graham Greene. New York: Viking, 1961. 179 pages.

—. *The Chronicles of Clovis.* New York: Viking, 1928. 242 pages.

—. *Collected Stories,* with an introduction by Christopher Morley and a biography by Saki's sister. New York: Modern Library, 1930. 718 pages.

—. *Incredible Tales,* ed. Richard Corbin and Ned E. Hoopes. New York: Dell, 1974.

Nabokov, Vladimir. *Nabokov's Dozen: A Collection of Thirteen Stories.* Garden City, New York: Doubleday, 1958. 214 pages.

—. *Nabokov's Quartet.* New York: Phaedra, 1966. 104 pages.

—. *A Russian Beauty and Other Stories,* tr. Dmitri Nabokov and Simon Karlinsky. New York: McGraw-Hill, 1973. 268 pages.

—. *Tyrants Destroyed, and Other Stories.* New York: McGraw-Hill, 1975. 238 pages.

Norris, Frank. *A Deal in Wheat and Other Stories of the New and Old West.* London: G. Richards, 1903. 272 pages.

Oates, Joyce Carol. *By the North Gate.* New York: Vanguard Press, 1963. 253 pages.

—. *Marriages and Infidelities.* New York: Vanguard Press, 1972. 497 pages.

—. *Upon the Sweeping Flood, and Other Stories.* New York: Vanguard Press, 1966. 250 pages.

—. *The Wheel of Love, and Other Stories.* New York: Vanguard Press, 1970. 440 pages.

Oates, Joyce Carol. *Where Are You Going, Where Have You Been?* Greenwich, Connecticut: Fawcett, 1974. 352 pages.

O'Brien, Fitz-James. *Collected Stories,* ed. and with an introduction by Edward J. O'Brien. New York: Boni, 1925. 240 pages.

O'Connor, Flannery. *The Complete Stories.* New York: Farrar, Straus and Giroux, 1971. 555 pages.

—. *Everything That Rises Must Converge.* New York: Farrar, Straus and Giroux, 1965. 269 pages.

O'Connor, Frank. *Crab Apple Jelly: Stories and Tales by Frank O'Connor.* New York: A. A. Knopf, 1944. 235 pages.

—. *More Stories by Frank O'Connor.* New York: A. A. Knopf, 1954. 385 pages.

—. *The Saint and Mary Kate.* New York: Macmillan, 1932. 301 pages.

—. *A Set of Variations: 27 Stories.* New York: A. A. Knopf, 1969. 338 pages.

—. *The Stories of Frank O'Connor.* New York: A. A. Knopf, 1952. 367 pages.

O'Flaherty, Liam. *Spring Sowing.* London: Jonathan Cape, Ltd., 1924. 287 pages.

—. *Wounded Cormorant and Other Stories,* with introduction by Vivian Mercier. New York: Norton, 1956.

O'Nolan, Brian. *The Best of Myles.* New York: Walker, 1968. 400 pages.

Paley, Grace. *Enormous Changes at the Last Minute.* New York: Farrar, Straus and Giroux, 1974. 198 pages.

—. *The Little Disturbances of Man.* New York: Viking, 1959. 187 pages.

Parker, Dorothy. *The Collected Stories of Dorothy Parker*, with a foreword by Franklin P. Adams. New York: Modern Library, 1942. 362 pages.

—. *The Portable Dorothy Parker*, ed. Brendan Gill. New York: Viking, 1944. 544 pages.

Peretz, Isaac Loeb. *Stories and Pictures*, tr. Helena Frank. Freeport, New York: Books for Libraries Press, 1971 reprint of 1906 edition. 455 pages.

Pirandello, Luigi. *Better Think Twice About It, and Twelve Other Stories*, tr. Arthur and Henrie Mayne. New York: E. P. Sutton and Company, Inc., 1934. 309 pages.

—. *Short Stories*, selected, translated, and edited by Frederick May. London and New York: Oxford University Press, 1965. 260 pages.

Poe, Edgar Allan. *The Complete Tales and Poems of Edgar Allan Poe*. New York: Modern Library, 1938. 1026 pages.

—. *The Complete Works of Edgar Allan Poe*. New York: Crowell, 1902. 16 vols.

—. *Introduction to Poe: A Thematic Reader*, ed. Eric W. Carlson. Glenview, Illinois: Scott, Foresman, 1967. 640 pages.

—. *The Portable Poe*, ed. Philip Van Doren Stern. New York: Viking, 1945. 666 pages.

—. *Selected Prose and Poetry*. New York: Rinehart, 1950. 528 pages.

—. *Seven Tales*. New York: Schocken Books, 1971. 245 pages.

—. *Tales of Edgar Allan Poe*. New York: Random House, 1944. 572 pages.

—. *The Works of Edgar Allan Poe*. New York: Funk and Wagnalls, 1904. 10 vols.

Porter, Katherine Anne. *The Collected Stories of Katherine

Anne Porter. New York: Harcourt, Brace and World, 1965. 495 pages.

Porter, Katherine Anne. *Flowering Judas and Other Stories.* New York: Harcourt, Brace, and World, 1953. 285 pages.

—. *The Leaning Tower and Other Stories.* New York: Harcourt, Brace, and World, 1944. 246 pages.

—. *Pale Horse, Pale Rider.* New York: Harcourt, Brace and World, 1939. 264 pages.

Powers, J. F. *The Presence of Grace.* Garden City, New York: Doubleday, 1956. 191 pages.

Pritchett, V. S. *Blind Love, and Other Stories.* New York: Random House, 1969. 247 pages.

—. *The Sailor, Sense of Humour, and Other Stories.* New York: A. A. Knopf, 1956. 369 pages.

—. *When My Girl Comes Home.* New York: A. A. Knopf, 1961. 241 pages.

Purdy, James. *Color of Darkness: Eleven Stories and a Novella.* New York: New Directions, 1957. 179 pages.

Pushkin, Alexander. *The Captain's Daughter, and Other Great Stories.* New York: Random House, 1936. 310 pages.

—. *Complete Prose Tales,* tr. Gillan R. Aitken. London: Barrie and Rickliff, 1966. 495 pages.

—. *The Poems, Prose and Plays by Alexander Pushkin.* New York: Modern Library, 1936. 896 pages.

Rawlings, Marjorie Kinnan. *The Marjorie Rawlings Reader.* New York: Scribner's, 1956. 504 pages.

Roth, Philip. *Goodbye Columbus and Five Short Stories.* Boston: Houghton Mifflin, 1959. 298 pages.

Runyon, Damon. *Best of Damon Runyon.* New York: Stokes,

1938. 318 pages.

Salinger, J. D. *Nine Stories.* Boston: Little, Brown, 1953. 302 pages.

Sansom, William. *The Stories of William Sansom.* Boston: Little, Brown, 1963. 421 pages.

Saroyan, William. *After Thirty Years: The Daring Young Man on the Flying Trapeze.* New York: Harcourt, Brace and World, 1964. 312 pages.

—. *The Assyrians, and Other Stories.* New York: Harcourt, Brace and World, 1950. 276 pages.

—. *Inhale and Exhale.* New York: Random House, 1936. 438 pages.

—. *My Name Is Aram.* New York: Harcourt, Brace and Company, 1940. 220 pages.

—. *The William Saroyan Reader.* New York: Braziller, 1958. 498 pages.

Sartre, Jean-Paul. *The Wall, and Other Stories*, tr. Lloyd Alexander. New York: New Directions, 1948. 270 pages.

Schnitzler, Arthur. *Stories and Plays by Arthur Schnitzler*, ed. and tr. by Allen W. Porterfield. Boston; New York: D. C. Heath and Company, 1930. 306 pages.

Schorer, Mark. *The State of Mind: Thirty-Two Stories.* Westport, Connecticut: Greenwood Press, reprint of 1947 edition. 346 pages.

Schwartz, Delmore. *In Dreams Begin Responsibilities.* New York: New Directions, 1938. 171 pages.

—. *Successful Love, and Other Stories.* New York: Corinth Books, 1961. 242 pages.

—. *The World Is a Wedding.* Norfolk, Connecticut: New Directions, 1948. 196 pages.

Scott, Sir Walter. *Short Stories by Sir Walter Scott.* St. Clair Shores, Michigan: Scholarly Press, 1970 reprint of 1934 edition. 339 pages.

Shaw, Irwin. *Act of Faith and Other Stories.* New York: Random House, 1946. 212 pages.

—. *Sailor off the Bremen, and Other Stories.* New York: Random House, 1939. 293 pages.

—. *Short Stories.* New York: Random House, 1966. 724 pages.

—. *Welcome to the City, and Other Stories.* New York: Random House, 1942. 269 pages.

Singer, Isaac Bashevis. *A Crown of Feathers.* New York: Farrar, Straus and Giroux, 1973. 342 pages.

—. *A Friend of Kafka, and Other Stories.* New York: Farrar, Straus and Giroux, 1970. 311 pages.

—. *Gimpel the Fool, and Other Stories.* New York: Noonday Press, 1957. 205 pages.

—. *An Isaac Bashevis Singer Reader.* New York: Farrar, Straus and Giroux, 1971. 560 pages.

—. *Seance, and Other Stories.* New York: Farrar, Straus and Giroux, 1968. 276 pages.

—. *Selected Short Stories.* New York: Modern Library, 1966. 379 pages.

—. *The Spinoza of Market Street, and Other Stories.* New York: Farrar, Straus, and Cudahy, 1961. 214 pages.

Solzhenitsyn, Alexander. *Stories and Prose Poems,* tr. Michael Glenny. New York: Farrar, Straus and Giroux, 1971. 267 pages.

Spark, Muriel. *Collected Stories.* London: Macmillan, 1967. 359 pages.

Spark, Muriel. *The Go-Away Bird, and Other Stories.* London: Macmillan, 1958. 214 pages.

Steele, Wilbur Daniel. *The Best Stories of Wilbur Daniel Steele.* Garden City, New York: Doubleday, 1946. 469 pages.

Stegner, Wallace. *The City of the Living, and Other Stories.* Boston: Houghton Mifflin, 1956. 206 pages.

Stein, Gertrude. *Selected Writings of Gertrude Stein,* ed. Carl Van Vechten. New York: Random House, 1946. 622 pages.

—. *Three Lives.* New York: Modern Library, 1933. 279 pages.

Steinbeck, John. *The Long Valley.* Cleveland: World Publishing Company, 1938. 303 pages.

—. *The Portable Steinbeck.* New York: Viking, 1946. 609 pages.

—. *The Red Pony.* New York: Viking Press, 1945. 120 pages.

Stephens, James. *The Crock of Gold.* New York: Macmillan, 1936. 298 pages.

—. *Etched in Moonlight.* New York: Macmillan, 1928. 199 pages.

—. *James Stephens Reader.* New York: Macmillan, 1962. 467 pages.

Stevenson, Robert Louis. *The Novels and Tales of Robert Louis Stevenson.* New York: Scribner's, 1918. 25 vols.

Stockton, Frank R. *Fables and Fiction: Frank Stockton.* Emmaus, Pennsylvania: Story Classics, 1949. 181 pages.

—. *The Lady, or the Tiger? and Other Stories.* New York: Scribner's, 1899. 201 pages.

—. *The Novels and Stories of Frank Stockton.* New York: Scribner's, 1899-1904. 23 vols.

Stuart, Jesse. *A Jesse Stuart Reader.* New York: Signet, n.d. 255 pages.

Suckow, Ruth. *Iowa Interiors.* New York: A. A. Knopf, 1926. 283 pages.

—. *Some Others and Myself: Seven Stories and a Memoir.* Westport, Connecticut: Greenwood Press, reprint of 1952 edition. 281 pages.

Tarkington, Booth. *The Works of Booth Tarkington.* Garden City, New York: Doubleday, Page, 1922-1924. 17 vols.

Taylor, Elizabeth. *Hester Lilly, and Twelve Short Stories.* New York: Viking, 1954. 210 pages.

Taylor, Peter. *The Collected Stories of Peter Taylor.* New York: Farrar, Straus and Giroux, 1968.

—. *Happy Families Are All Alike.* New York: McDowell, Obolensky, 1959. 305 pages.

—. *A Long Fourth, and Other Stories.* New York: Harcourt Brace, 1948. 166 pages.

—. *Miss Leonora When Last Seen, and Fifteen Other Stories.* New York: Obolensky, 1963. 398 pages.

Thomas, Dylan. *Adventures in the Skin Trade, and Other Stories.* New York: New Directions, 1964. 275 pages.

—. *The Map of Love.* London: Dent, 1939. 115 pages.

Thurber, James. *My Life and Hard Times.* New York and London: Harper and Row, 1933. 153 pages.

—. *My World and Welcome to It.* New York: Harcourt and Brace and Company, 1942. 310 pages.

—. *The Thurber Carnival.* New York and London: Harper and Brothers, 1945. 369 pages.

Tolstoy, Leo. *The Death of Ivan Ilyich, and Other Stories.* London: W. Heinemann, 1902. 362 pages.

Tolstoy, Leo. *Great Short Works of Leo Tolstoy.* New York: Harper-Row, 1967. 685 pages.

—. *What Men Live By.* New York: Pantheon Books, 1943. 223 pages.

Toomer, Jean. *Cane.* New York: Harper and Row, 1923. 239 pages.

Turgenev, Ivan. *The District Doctor, and Other Stories.* Emmaus, Pennsylvania: Story Classics, 1951. 206 pages.

—. *Selected Tales of Ivan Turgenev.* Garden City, New York: Doubleday, 1960. 335 pages.

—. *The Vintage Turgenev.* New York: Vintage Books, 1964, c1950. 2 vols.

Twain, Mark. *The Complete Short Stories of Mark Twain,* ed. Charles Neider. Garden City, New York: Hanover House, 1957. 676 pages.

—. *The Portable Mark Twain,* ed. Bernard De Voto. New York: Viking, 1946. 790 pages.

Unamuno, Miguel de. *Abel Sanchez and Other Stories,* tr. and with introduction by Anthony Kerrigan. Chicago: Henry Regnery, 1956. 267 pages.

Updike, John. *Assorted Prose.* New York: A. A. Knopf, 1965. 326 pages.

—. *Museums and Women and Other Stories.* New York: A. A. Knopf, 1972. 282 pages.

—. *The Music School.* New York: A. A. Knopf, 1966. 259 pages.

—. *Olinger Stories.* New York: Vintage Press, 1964. 191 pages.

—. *Pigeon Feathers, and Other Stories.* New York: A. A. Knopf,

1962. 278 pages.

Updike, John. *The Same Door.* New York: A. A. Knopf, 1959. 241 pages.

Verga, Giovanni. *Cavalleria Rusticana and Other Narratives.* Emmaus, Pennsylvania: Story Classics, 1950. 173 pages.

—. *The She-Wolf and Other Stories,* tr. and ed. Giovanni Cecchetti. Berkeley: University of California Press, 1973. 299 pages.

Warren, Robert Penn. *The Circus in the Attic, and Other Stories.* New York: Harcourt Brace, 1947. 276 pages.

Wells, H. G. *Complete Short Stories.* London: Benn, 1966. 1038 pages.

Welty, Eudora. *The Bride of the Innisfallen, and Other Stories.* New York: Harcourt Brace, 1955. 207 pages.

—. *A Curtain of Green, and Other Stories.* New York: Harcourt, Brace, 1941. 289 pages.

—. *The Golden Apples.* New York: Harcourt, Brace and World, 1949. 277 pages.

—. *Selected Stories.* New York: Modern Library, 1943. 2 vols.

—. *Thirteen Stories by Eudora Welty,* with introduction by Ruth M. Vande Kieft. New York: Harcourt, Brace and World, 1965. 243 pages.

—. *The Wide Net and Other Stories.* New York: Harcourt, Brace and Company, 1943. 214 pages.

Wescott, Glenway. *Good-Bye Wisconsin.* New York: Harper and Brothers, 1928. 158 pages.

—. *The Grandmothers.* New York and London: Harper and Brothers, 1927. 388 pages.

Wharton, Edith. *Best Short Stories.* New York: Scribner's,

1958. 292 pages.

Wharton, Edith. *Collected Short Stories*, ed. R. W. B. Lewis. New York, 1968. 2 vols.

—. *The Edith Wharton Reader*, ed. Louis Auchincloss. New York: Scribner's, 1965. 700 pages.

—. *The Greater Inclination*. New York: Scribner's, 1899. 254 pages.

—. *Roman Fever, and Other Stories*. New York: Scribner's, 1964. 238 pages.

—. *Tales of Men and Ghosts*. New York: Scribner's, 1910. 438 pages.

White, E. B. *An E. B. White Reader*, ed. William W. Watt and Robert W. Bradford. New York: Harper-Row, 1966. 342 pages.

Williams, William Carlos. *The Farmers' Daughters: Collected Stories*. Norfolk, Connecticut: New Directions, 1961. 374 pages.

—. *The William Carlos Williams Reader*, ed. and with introduction by M. L. Rosenthal. Norfolk, Connecticut: New Directions, 1966. 412 pages.

Wister, Owen. *The West of Owen Wister: Selected Short Stories*, ed. Robert L. Hough. Lincoln: University of Nebraska Press, 1972. 247 pages.

Wolfe, Thomas. *From Death to Morning*. New York: Scribner's, 1935. 304 pages.

—. *The Hills Beyond*. New York and London: Harper and Brothers, 1941. 386 pages.

—. *The Portable Thomas Wolfe*. New York: Viking, 1946. 712 pages.

—. *The Thomas Wolfe Reader*. New York: Scribner's, 1962.

690 pages.

Woolf, Virginia. *A Haunted House and Other Short Stories by Virginia Woolf.* New York: Harcourt, Brace and Company, 1944. 148 pages.

Wright, Richard. *Eight Men.* New York: Pyramid Books, 1961. 204 pages.

Zweig, Stefan. *Passion and Pain,* tr. Eden and Cedar Paul. Freeport, New York: Books for Libraries Press, 1971 reprint of 1925 edition. 273 pages.

II A. CROSS-INDEX, SHORT-STORY AUTHORS
AND THEIR CRITICS

(See relevant book entries in II B)

Agee, James	Erling Larsen Peter H. Ohlin
Aiken, Conrad	Frederick J. Hoffmann Jay Martin
Aleichem, Sholom	Maurice Samuel Marie Waife-Goldberg
Anderson, Sherwood	David D. Anderson Irving Howe Walter B. Rideout James Erwin Schevill Brom Weber
Babel, Isaac	Patricia Carden James E. Falen
Baldwin, James	Kenneth Kinnamon
Balzac, Honoré de	Philippe Bertault André Maurois
Barth, John	Gerhard Joseph
Baudelaire, Charles-Pierre	Emil Starkie Martin Turnell
Beckett, Samuel	A. Alvarez Martin Esslin Melvin J. Friedman

Beckett, Samuel (cont'd)	Frederick J. Hoffman Hugh Kenner Michael Robinson George H. Szanto Katharine Worth
Beerbohm, Max	Samuel N. Behrman Lord David Cecil
Bellow, Saul	Robert Detweiler Irving Malin Earl Rovit Brigitte Scheer-Schäzler Nathan A. Scott, Jr.
Bennett, Arnold	Dudley Barker John D. Gordon John Lucas John Wain
Bierce, Ambrose	Richard O'Connor
Borges, Jorge Luis	Ana Maria Barranechea Martin S. Stabb
Bowen, Elizabeth	Jocelyn Brooke
Cable, George Washington	Louis D. Rubin, Jr. Arlin Turner
Caldwell, Erskine	James Korges
Camus, Albert	Germaine Brée Donald Lazere Albert Maquet Emmett Parker Felix S. A. Rysten Philip Thody
Capote, Truman	Craig M. Goad William L. Nance
Cather, Willa	Mildred R. Bennett

Cather, Willa (cont'd)	E. K. Brown and Leon Edel
	David Daiches
	Elizabeth Shepley Sergeant
	Bernice Slote and Virginia Faulkner
	David Stouck
	James Woodress
Chekhov, Anton	Walter H. Bruford
	William Gerhardi
	Ronald Hingley
	Robert Louis Jackson
	David Magarshack
	Ernest J. Simmons
	Logan Speirs
	Jane Wexford
	Thomas Winner
Chesterton, G. K.	Hilaire Belloc
Clark, Walter Van Tilburg	Max Westbrook
Conrad, Joseph	Wilfred S. Dowden
	John D. Gordan
	Lawrence Graver
	Bruce Johnson
	Frederick R. Karl
	Marvin Mudrick
	Royal Roussel
	Norman Sherry
Crane, Stephen	Maurice Bassan
	Thomas Beer
	John Berryman
	Jean Cazemajou
	Donald B. Gibson
	Milne Holton
	Joseph Katz
	Eric Solomon
	R. W. Stallman
	Richard M. Weatherford
Daudet, Alphonse	Murray Sachs

Gide, André (cont'd)	Justin O'Brien George D. Painter
Glasgow, Ellen	Louis Auchincloss
Gogol, Nikolai	Janko Lavrin David Magarshack Vsevolod Setchkarev
Goldsmith, Oliver	Ricardo Quintana G. S. Rousseau
Gordon, Caroline	Thomas H. Landess Frederick P. W. McDowell W. J. Stuckey
Gorky, Maxim	Dan Levin Irwin Weil
Greene, Graham	Robert O. Evans Samuel Hynes
Hardy, Thomas	R. G. Cox Albert J. Guerard Evelyn Hardy Irving Howe J. Hillis Miller Carl J. Weber
Harris, Joel Chandler	Paul M. Cousins
Harte, Bret	George R. Stewart
Hauptmann, Gerhart	Hugh F. Garten
Hawthorne, Nathaniel	Millicent Bell Agnes McNeill Donohue Neal F. Doubleday Richard Harter Fogle A. N. Kaul Mary Rohrberger Hyatt H. Waggoner

Jewett, Sarah Orne	Richard Cary
	F. O. Matthiessen
	Margaret F. Thorp
Joyce, James	James R. Baker and Thomas F. Staley
	Edward Brandabur
	Homer O. Brown
	William Chace
	Richard K. Cross
	R. H. Deming
	Richard Ellmann
	Peter K. Garrett
	Don Gifford and Robert Seidman
	Herbert Gorman
	Harry Levin
	A. Walton Litz
	A Reader's Guide to James Joyce
	Robert Scholes and A. Walton Litz
	William York Tindall
Kafka, Franz	Wilhelm Emrich
	Ronald D. Gray
	Calvin S. Hall and Richard E. Lind
	Erich Heller
	Charles Neider
	George H. Szanto
	Herbert Tauber
Kipling, Rudyard	Bonamy Dobrée
	Elliot L. Gilbert
	Andrew Rutherford
	J. I. M. Stewart
Kleist, Heinrich Von	Walter Sitz
La Farge, Oliver	T. M. Pearce
Lagerkvist, Pär	Winston Weathers

Mansfield, Katherine	Sylvia Berkman Saralyn R. Daly Marvin Magalaner
Maugham, Somerset	Laurence Brander Richard A. Cordell
Maupassant, Guy de	Artine Artinian Ernest Boyd Paul Ignotus Francis Steegmuller
Melville, Herman	Darrel Abel Watson G. Branch Daniel Buerger Richard V. Chase Richard Harter Fogle Arthur Golden James E. Miller, Jr. Felix S. A. Rysten Kingsley Widmer
Mérimée, Prosper	André Billy Frank Paul Bowman
Moore, George	Graham Owens
Moravia, Alberto	Jane E. Cottrell Giuliano Dego Donald Heiney Joan Ross and Donald Freed
H. H. Munro ("Saki")	Charles H. Gillen
Nabokov, Vladimir	Alfred Appel and Charles Newman L. S. Dembo Andrew Field William W. Rowe
Norris, Frank	William B. Dillingham Warren French

Poe, Edgar Allan (cont'd)	Edward Wagenknecht J. Walsh
Porter, Katherine Anne	Lodwick Hartley and George Core George Hendrich M. M. Liberman Ray B. West, Jr.
Powers, J. F.	John V. Hagopian
Purdy, James	Bettina Schwarzschild
Pushkin, Alexander	Samuel H. Cross and Ernest J. Simmons Janko Lavrin D. S. Mirsky
Rilke, Rainer Maria	H. W. Belmore Eliza M. Butler
Robbe-Grillet, Alain	George H. Szanto

Salinger, J. D.	William F. Belcher and
	    James W. Lee
	Warren French
	Frederick L. Gwynn and
	    Joseph L. Blotner
	Kenneth Hamilton
	Marvin Laser and
	    Norman Fruman
	James E. Miller, Jr.
	Arthur Mizener

Sartre, Jean-Paul	Edith Kern
Schnitzler, Arthur	Herbert Reicher and Herman Salinger
Scott, Sir Walter	Norman Jeffares
Singer, Isaac Bashevis	Irving Malin Ben Siegel

Turgenev, Ivan	J. A. T. Lloyd
	Avrahm Yarmolinsky
Twain, Mark	Frederick Anderson
	Van Wyck Brooks
	James M. Cox
	Arthur L. Scott
	Henry Nash Smith
	John S. Tuckey
Unamuno, Miguel de	Paul Ilie
Updike, John	Rachel C. Butchard
	Alice and Kenneth Hamilton
	Kenneth Hamilton
	The New York Times editors
	Charles Thomas Samuels
	Larry E. Taylor
Verga, Giovanni	Thomas G. Bergin
Warren, Robert Penn	Leonard Casper
	J. L. Longley, Jr.
	Paul West
Wells, H. G.	Bernard Bergonzi
	Alfred Borello
	Patrick Parrinder
Welty, Eudora	Joseph A. Bryant
	Ruth M. Vande Kieft
Wescott, Glenway	Ira D. Johnson
Wharton, Edith	Louis Auchincloss
	Olivia Coolidge
	Irving Howe
	Blake Nevius
Williams, William Carlos	James E. Breslin
	James Guimond
	Vivienne Koch
	J. Hillis Miller

II B. CRITICS OF SHORT-STORY AUTHORS

(See first the cross-index, part II A)

Abel, Darrel. *A Simplified Approach to Herman Melville.* Great Neck, New York: Barron's Educational Series, 1964. 51 pages.

Alvarez, Alfred. *Samuel Beckett.* New York: Viking, 1973. 128 pages.

Anderson, David D. *Sherwood Anderson: An Introduction and Interpretation.* New York: Barnes and Noble, 1967. 182 pages.

Anderson, Frederick, ed. *Mark Twain: The Critical Heritage.* New York: Barnes and Noble, 1971. 347 pages.

Andreas, Osborn. *Henry James and the Expanding Horizon: A Study of the Meaning and Basic Themes of James' Fiction.* Westport, Connecticut: Greenwood Press, reprint of 1948 edition. 179 pages.

Artinian, Artine. *Maupassant Criticism in France.* New York: Russell and Russell, 1969, c1941. 228 pages.

Auchincloss, Louis. *Edith Wharton.* Minneapolis, University of Minnesota Press, 1961. 46 pages.

—. *Edith Wharton: A Woman in Her Time.* New York: Viking, 1971.

—. *Ellen Glasgow.* Minneapolis, University of Minnesota Press, 1964. 48 pages.

Axelrad, Jacob. *Anatole France: A Life Without Illusions,*

1844-1924. New York and London: Harper and Brothers, 1944. 480 pages.

Baker, Carlos. *Hemingway: The Writer as Artist.* Princeton, New Jersey: Princeton University Press, 1963. 379 pages.

Baker, James R. and Thomas F. Staley, eds. *James Joyce's Dubliners: A Critical Handbook.* Belmont, California: Wadsworth, 1969. 188 pages.

Barker, Dudley. *Writer by Trade: A Portrait of Arnold Bennett.* London and New York: Atheneum, 1966. 260 pages.

Barranechea, Ana Maria. *Borges: The Labyrinth Maker,* ed. and tr. Robert Limes, New York, 1965.

Bart, Benjamin. *Flaubert.* Syracuse, New York: Syracuse University Press, 1967. 791 pages.

Bassan, Maurice, ed. *Stephen Crane: A Collection of Critical Essays.* Englewood Cliffs, New Jersey: Prentice-Hall, 1967. 184 pages.

Bassett, John, ed. *William Faulkner: The Critical Heritage.* London, Boston: Routledge and Kegan Paul, 1975. 438 pages.

Baumer, Franz. *Hermann Hesse,* tr. John Conway. New York: Ungar, 1969. 107 pages.

Beach, Joseph Warren. *The Method of Henry James.* Philadelphia: A. Saifer, 1954. 299 pages.

Beer, Thomas. *Stephen Crane: A Study in American Letters.* New York: Farrar, Straus, and Giroux, reprint of 1923 edition. 248 pages.

Behrman, Samuel N. *Portrait of Max [Beerbohm].* New York: Random House, 1960. 317 pages. (Published in London, 1960, as *Conversation with Max.*)

Belcher, William F., and James W. Lee, eds. *J. D. Salinger and the Critics.* Belmont, California: Wadsworth, 1962. 179

pages.

Bell, Millicent. *Hawthorne's View of the Artist.* Albany, New York: State University of New York, 1962. 214 pages.

Belmore, H. W. *Rilke's Craftsmanship.* New York and London: Oxford University Press, 1954. 234 pages.

Bennett, Mildred R. *The World of Willa Cather.* New York: Dodd, Mead, 1951. 226 pages.

Benson, Jackson, ed. *Hemingway in Our Time.* Corvallis, Oregon: Oregon State University Press, 1974. 214 pages.

Bergin, Thomas Goddard. *Giovanni Verga.* New Haven: Yale University Press, 1931. 135 pages.

Bergonzi, Bernard. *The Early H. G. Wells: A Study of the Scientific Romances.* Toronto: University of Toronto Press, 1961. 226 pages.

Berkman, Sylvia. *Katherine Mansfield: A Critical Study.* New Haven: Yale University Press, 1951. 246 pages.

Berryman, John. *Stephen Crane.* New York: Farrar, Straus, and Giroux, 1950. 347 pages.

Bertault, Philippe. *Balzac and the Human Comedy.* New York: New York University Press, 1963. 212 pages.

Billy, Andre. *Mérimée.* Paris: Flammarion, 1959. 364 pages.

Bone, Robert A. *Richard Wright.* Minneapolis, University of Minnesota Press, 1956. 48 pages.

Bowden, Edwin T. *The Themes of Henry James.* New Haven: Yale University Press, 1956. 117 pages.

Bowman, Frank Paul. *Prosper Mérimée: Heroism, Pessimism, and Irony.* Berkeley: University of California Press, 1962. 205 pages.

Boyd, Ernest. *Guy de Maupassant.* New York and London:

A. A. Knopf, 1926. 258 pages.

Bradbury, Malcolm, ed. *Forster: A Collection of Critical Essays.* Englewood Cliffs, New Jersey: Prentice-Hall, 1966. 180 pages.

Branch, Watson G., ed. *Melville: The Critical Heritage.* Boston and London: Routledge and Kegan Paul, 1974. 444 pages.

Brandabur, Edward. *A Scrupulous Meanness: A Study of Joyce's Early Work.* Urbana, Illinois: University of Illinois Press, 1971. 184 pages.

Brander, Laurence. *Somerset Maugham: A Guide.* Edinburgh: Oliver and Boyd, 1963. 222 pages.

Brée, Germaine. *Camus.* New Brunswick, New Jersey: Rutgers University Press, 1961. 281 pages.

—. *Camus: A Collection of Critical Essays.* Englewood Cliffs, New Jersey: Prentice-Hall, 1962. 182 pages.

Breslin, James E. *William Carlos Williams: An American Artist.* New York and London; Oxford University Press, 1970. 246 pages.

Brignano, Russell Carl. *Richard Wright: An Introduction to the Man and His Works.* Pittsburgh: Pittsburgh University Press, 1970. 201 pages.

Brod, Max. *Heinrich Heine: The Artist in Revolt.* New York: New York University Press, 1957. 355 pages.

Brooke, Jocelyn. *Aldous Huxley.* London: Longmans, Green, 1954. 31 pages.

—. *Elizabeth Bowen.* London: Longmans, Green, 1952. 32 pages.

Brooks, Van Wyck. *The Ordeal of Mark Twain.* New York: E. P. Dutton and Company, 1920. 267 pages.

Broussard, Louis. *The Measure of Poe.* Norman: University of

Oklahoma Press, 1969. 168 pages.

Brown, Edward Killoran, and Leon Edel. *Willa Cather: A Critical Biography.* New York: A. A. Knopf, 1953. 351 pages.

Brown, Homer O. *James Joyce's Early Fiction: The Biography of a Form.* Cleveland, Ohio: Case Western Reserve University Press, 1972. 272 pages.

Bruford, Walter H. *Chekhov and His Russia: A Sociological Study.* London: K. Paul, Trench, Trubner, 1947. 233 pages.

Bryant, Joseph A. *Eudora Welty.* Minneapolis: University of Minnesota Press, 1968. 48 pages.

Bucco, Martin. *Wilbur Daniel Steele.* New York: Twayne, 1972. 186 pages.

Buck, Stratton. *Gustave Flaubert.* New York: Twayne, 1966. 153 pages.

Buitenhis, Peter. *The Grasping Imagination: The American Writings of Henry James.* Toronto: University of Toronto Press, 1970. 288 pages.

Burg, David, and George Feifer. *Solzhenitsyn: A Biography.* New York: Stein and Day, 1972. 371 pages.

Butchard, Rachael C. *John Updike: Yea Saying.* Carbondale: Southern Illinois University, 1971.

Butler, Eliza M. *Rainer Maria Rilke.* New York: Farrar, Straus and Giroux, reprint of 1941 edition. 437 pages.

Campbell, Killis. *The Mind of Poe.* Cambridge: Harvard University Press, 1933. 237 pages.

Carden, Patricia. *The Art of Isaac Babel.* Ithaca: Cornell University Press, 1972. 223 pages.

Carlson, Eric W., ed. *The Recognition of Edgar Allan Poe: Selected Criticism Since 1829.* Ann Arbor: University of

Michigan Press, 1966. 316 pages.

Cary, Richard. *Sarah Orne Jewett.* New York: Twayne, 1962. 175 pages.

Casper, Leonard. *Robert Penn Warren: The Dark and Bloody Ground.* Westport, Connecticut: Greenwood Press, reprint of 1960 edition. 212 pages.

Cazemajou, Jean. *Stephen Crane.* Minneapolis: University of Minnesota Press, 1969. 47 pages.

Cecil, Lord David. *Max [Beerbohm]: A Biography.* London: Constable, 1964, and Boston: Houghton-Mifflin, 1965. 507 pages.

Chace, William George, ed. *Joyce: A Collection of Critical Essays.* Englewood Cliffs, New Jersey: Prentice-Hall, 1974. 184 pages.

Chase, Richard V., ed. *Melville: A Collection of Critical Essays.* Englewood Cliffs, New Jersey: Prentice-Hall, 1962. 168 pages.

Christian, R. F. *Tolstoy: A Critical Introduction.* London: Cambridge University Press, 1969. 291 pages.

Clemons, Walter. *Joyce Carol Oates: Love and Violence, A Vision of America.* Greenwich, Connecticut: Fawcett, 1972. 10 pages.

Cobb, Palmer. *The Influence of E. T. A. Hoffman on the Tales of Edgar Allan Poe.* Chapel Hill, North Carolina: The University of North Carolina Press, 1908. 104 pages.

Colmer, John. *E. M. Forster: The Personal Voice.* Boston and London: Routledge and Kegan Paul, 1975. 256 pages.

Consolo, Dominick, compiler. *D. H. Lawrence: "The Rocking-Horse Winner."* Columbus, Ohio: Merrill, 1969.

Coolidge, Olivia. *Edith Wharton.* New York: Scribner's, 1964. 221 pages.

Cordell, Richard A. *Somerset Maugham, A Writer for All Seasons: A Biographical and Critical Study.* Bloomington, Indiana: Indiana University Press, 1969. 308 pages.

Cottrell, Jane E. *Alberto Moravia.* New York: Ungar, 1974. 166 pages.

Cousins, Paul M. *Joel Chandler Harris: A Biography.* Baton Rouge, Louisiana: Louisiana State University Press, 1968. 237 pages.

Cox, Charles B., ed. *Dylan Thomas: A Collection of Critical Essays.* Englewood Cliffs, New Jersey: Prentice-Hall, 1966. 186 pages.

—. *Joseph Conrad: The Modern Imagination.* New York: Rowman and Littlefield, 1974. 191 pages.

Cox, James M. *Mark Twain: The Fate of Humor.* Princeton, New Jersey: Princeton University Press, 1966. 321 pages.

Cox, R. G., ed. *Thomas Hardy: The Critical Heritage.* Boston and London: Routledge and Kegan Paul, 1975.

Cross, K. G. W. *F. Scott Fitzgerald.* Edinburgh: Oliver and Boyd, 1964. 120 pages.

Cross, Richard K. *Flaubert and Joyce.* Princeton: Princeton University Press, 1971. 195 pages.

Cross, Samuel H., and Ernest J. Simmons, eds. *Centennial Essays for Pushkin.* New York: Russell and Russell, 1967, c1964. 226 pages.

Daiches, David. *Robert Louis Stevenson.* Norfolk, Connecticut: New Directions, 1947. 196 pages.

—. *Virginia Woolf.* Norfolk, Connecticut: New Directions, 1963. 169 pages.

—. *Willa Cather: A Critical Introduction.* Ithaca, New York: Cornell University Press, 1951. 193 pages.

Daly, Saralyn R. *Katherine Mansfield.* New York: Twayne, 1965. 143 pages.

Davidson, Edward Hutchins. *Poe: A Critical Study.* Cambridge, Massachusetts: Harvard University Press, 1957. 296 pages.

Davis, Robert M., ed. *Steinbeck: A Collection of Critical Essays.* Englewood Cliffs, New Jersey: Prentice-Hall, 1972. 183 pages.

Dego, Giuliano. *Moravia.* New York: Barnes and Noble, 1967, c1966. 120 pages.

Dembo, L. S., ed. *Nabokov: The Man and His Work.* Madison: University of Wisconsin Press, 1967. 282 pages.

Deming, R. H., ed. *James Joyce: The Critical Heritage,* 2 vols. (821 pages). Boston and London: Routledge and Kegan Paul, 1970.

Detweiler, Robert. *Saul Bellow.* Grand Rapids: Eerdmans, 1967. 48 pages.

Dillingham, William B. *Frank Norris: Instinct and Art.* Lincoln: University of Nebraska, 1969. 185 pages.

Dobree, Bonamy. *Rudyard Kipling.* London: Longmans, 1966. 56 pages.

Donohue, Agnes McNeill, ed. *A Casebook on the Hawthorne Question.* New York: Crowell, 1963. 347 pages.

Dooley, D. J. *The Art of Sinclair Lewis.* Lincoln: University of Nebraska Press, 1967. 286 pages.

Doubleday, Neal F. *Hawthorne's Early Tales, a Critical Study.* Durham, North Carolina: Duke University Press, 1972. 262 pages.

Dowden, Wildred S. *Joseph Conrad: The Imaged Style.* Nashville: Vanderbilt University Press, 1970. 200 pages.

Doyle, Paul A. *Liam O'Flaherty.* New York: Twayne, 1971.

154 pages.

Doyle, Paul A. *Sean O'Faolain.* New York: Twayne, 1968. 156 pages.

Drake, Robert. *Flannery O'Connor.* Grand Rapids, Michigan: Eerdmans, 1966. 48 pages.

Draper, R. P., ed. *Lawrence: The Critical Heritage.* Boston and London: Routledge and Kegan Paul, 1975.

Dupee, F. W., ed. *The Question of Henry James.* New York: Farrar, Straus and Giroux, 1945. 302 pages.

Eble, Kenneth E., ed. *Howells: A Century of Criticism.* Dallas: Southern Methodist University Press, 1962. 247 pages.

Edel, Leon. *Henry James,* 4 vols. Philadelphia and London: Hart-Davis, 1953, 1962, 1969.

Edel, Leon, ed. *Henry James: A Collection of Critical Essays.* Englewood Cliffs, New Jersey: Prentice-Hall, 1963. 185 pages.

Eggenschwiler, David. *The Christian Humanism of Flannery O'Connor.* Detroit, Michigan: Wayne State University Press, 1972. 148 pages.

Elder, Donald. *Ring Lardner.* Garden City, New York: Doubleday, 1956. 409 pages.

Elias, Robert Henry. *Theodore Dreiser: Apostle of Nature.* New York: A. A. Knopf, 1949. 402 pages.

Ellis, Elmer. *Mr. Dooley's America: A Life of Finley Peter Dunne.* New York: Knopf, 1941. 349 pages.

Ellmann, Richard. *James Joyce.* New York and London: Oxford University Press, 1959. 842 pages.

Emanuel, James. *Langston Hughes.* New York: Twayne, 1967. 192 pages.

Emery, Clark. *The World of Dylan Thomas.* London: Dent, 1971. 319 pages.

Emrich, Wilhelm. *Franz Kafka: A Critical Study of His Writings.* New York: Ungar, 1968. 561 pages.

Erling, Larsen. *James Agee.* Minneapolis: University of Minnesota Press, 1971. 48 pages.

Esslin, Martin, ed. *Samuel Beckett: A Collection of Critical Essays.* Englewood Cliffs, New Jersey: Prentice-Hall, 1965. 182 pages.

Evans, Robert O., ed. *Graham Greene: Some Critical Considerations.* Lexington: University of Kentucky Press, 1973.

Everett, Walter K. *Faulkner's Art and Characters.* Woodbury, New York: Barron's Educational Series, 1969. 305 pages.

Falen, James E. *Isaac Babel, Russian Master of the Short Story.* Knoxville: University of Tennessee Press, 1974. 270 pages.

Feeley, Kathleen. *Flannery O'Connor: Voice of the Peacock.* New Brunswick, New Jersey: Rutgers University Press, 1972. 198 pages.

Feuerlicht, Ignace. *Thomas Mann.* New York: Twayne, 1968. 177 pages.

Field, A. Leslie, and Joyce W., eds. *Bernard Malamud and the Critics.* New York: New York University Press, 1970. 353 pages.

Field, Andrew. *Nabokov: His Life in Art.* London: Holder and Stoughton, 1967. 397 pages.

Fogle, Richard Harter. *Hawthorne's Fiction: The Light and the Dark.* Norman: University of Oklahoma Press, 1964. 256 pages.

—. *Melville's Shorter Tales.* Norman: University of Oklahoma Press, 1966. 150 pages.

Foner, Philip S. *Jack London, American Rebel.* New York: Citadel Press, 1964. 155 pages.

Forster, E. M. *Virginia Woolf.* New York: Harcourt Brace, 1942. 40 pages.

Foster, Edward. *Mary E. Wilkins Freeman.* New York: Hendricks House, 1956. 229 pages.

Fowlie, Wallace. *André Gide: His Life and Art.* New York: Collier Books, 1966. 217 pages.

Freeman, Mary. *D. H. Lawrence: A Basic Study of His Ideas.* New York: Grosset and Dunlap, 1961. 277 pages.

French, Warren. *Frank Norris.* New Haven, Connecticut; New York: Twayne, 1973, c1962. 160 pages.

—. *J. D. Salinger.* New York: Twayne, 1963. 191 pages.

—. *John Steinbeck.* New York: Twayne, 1961. 190 pages.

Friedman, Melvin J., and Lewis A. Lawson, eds. *The Added Dimension: The Art and Mind of Flannery O'Connor.* New York: Fordham University Press, 1966. 309 pages.

Friedman, Melvin J., ed. *Samuel Beckett Now,* Second Edition. Chicago: University of Chicago Press, 1975. 275 pages.

Friedrich, Otto. *Ring Lardner.* Minneapolis: University of Minnesota Press, 1973. 48 pages.

Frohock, W. M. *Frank Norris.* Minneapolis: University of Minnesota Press, 1973. 48 pages.

—. *Theodore Dreiser.* Minneapolis: University of Minnesota Press, 1973. 48 pages.

Gardner, Philip, ed. *E. M. Forster: The Critical Heritage.* London and Boston: Routledge and Kegan Paul, 1973. 498 pages.

Garrett, Peter K., ed. *Twentieth-Century Interpretations of*

Dubliners: A Collection of Critical Essays.   Englewood Cliffs, New Jersey: Prentice-Hall, 1968. 119 pages.

Garten, Hugh F. *Gerhart Hauptmann.* New Haven: Yale University Press, 1954. 72 pages.

Gerber, Philip L. *Theodore Dreiser.* New York: Twayne, 1964. 220 pages.

Gerhardi, William Alexander. *Antón Chekhov: A Critical Study.* New York: Duffield and Company, 1923. 207 pages.

Gibson, Donald B. *The Fiction of Stephen Crane.* Carbondale: Southern Illinois University Press, 1966, c1962. 261 pages.

Gifford, Don, and Robert Seidman. *Notes for Joyce: Dubliners and A Portrait of the Artist as a Young Man.* New York: Dutton, 1967. 187 pages.

Gilbert, Elliot L. *The Good Kipling: Studies in the Short Story.* Athens, Ohio: Ohio University Press, 1971, c1970. 216 pages.

—. *Kipling and the Critics.* New York: New York University Press, 1965. 183 pages.

Gillen, Charles H. *H. H. Munro* ("Saki"). New York: Twayne, 1969. 178 pages.

Giraud, Raymond, ed. *Flaubert: A Collection of Critical Essays.* Englewood Cliffs, New Jersey: Prentice-Hall, 1964. 180 pages.

Giudice, Gaspare. *Luigi Pirandello.* Torino: Unione Tipografico-Editrice Torinese, 1963. 566 pages.

Goad, Craig M. *Daylight and Darkness, Dream and Delusion: The Works of Truman Capote.* Emporia, Kansas: Emporia State Research Studies, 1967. 57 pages.

Golden, Arthur, ed. *Herman Melville: A Collection of Criticism.* New York: McGraw-Hill, 1975.

Gordon, John D. *Arnold Bennett: The Centenary of His Birth.* New York: New York Public Library, 1968. Berg Collection of Works.

—. *Joseph Conrad: The Making of a Novelist.* New York: Russell and Russell, 1963, c1940. 430 pages.

Gorman, Herbert. *James Joyce.* New York: Farrar Straus and Grioux, reprint of 1939 edition. 358 pages.

Gransden, Karl W. *E. M. Forster.* Edinburgh: Oliver and Boyd, 1962. 120 pages.

Graver, Lawrence. *Carson McCullers.* Minneapolis: University of Minnesota Press, 1969. 48 pages.

—. *Conrad's Short Fiction.* Berkeley: University of California Press, 1969. 239 pages.

Gray, James. *John Steinbeck.* Minneapolis: University of Minnesota Press, 1971. 48 pages.

Gray, Ronald D., ed. *Kafka: A Collection of Critical Essays.* Englewood Cliffs, New Jersey: Prentice-Hall, 1962. 182 pages.

Grebstein, Sheldon Norman. *Sinclair Lewis.* New York: Twayne, 1962. 192 pages.

Gregory, Horace. *D. H. Lawrence: Pilgrim of the Apocalypse.* New York: Grove Press, 1957. 118 pages.

Griffin, Martin J. *Frank R. Stockton: A Critical Biography.* Philadelphia: University of Pennsylvania, 1939. 178 pages.

Griffith, Albert J. *Peter Taylor.* New York: Twayne, 1970. 183 pages.

Guerard, Albert J. *André Gide.* Cambridge: Harvard University Press, 1951. 263 pages.

—, ed. *Hardy: A Collection of Critical Essays.* Englewood Cliffs, New Jersey: Prentice-Hall, 1963. 180 pages.

Guerard, Albert J., ed. *Thomas Hardy.* New York: New Directions, 1964. 207 pages.

Guiguet, Jean. *Virginia Woolf and Her Works.* London: Hogarth Press, 1965. 487 pages.

Guimond, James. *William Carlos Williams: A Developmental Study.* Ann Arbor: University of Michigan, 1966. 370 pages.

Gwynn, Frederick L., and Joseph L. Blotner, eds. *The Fiction of J. D. Salinger.* Pittsburgh: University of Pittsburgh Press, 1958. 59 pages.

Hagopian, John V. *J. F. Powers.* New York: Twayne, 1968. 174 pages.

Hall, Calvin S., and Richard E. Lind. *Dreams, Life, and Literature: A Study of Franz Kafka.* Chapel Hill: University of North Carolina Press, 1970. 133 pages.

Hamilton, Alice and Kenneth. *The Elements of John Updike.* Grand Rapids, Michigan: Eerdmans, 1970. 267 pages.

Hamilton, Kenneth. *John Updike.* Grand Rapids, Michigan: Eerdmans, 1967. 47 pages.

—. *J. D. Salinger.* Grand Rapids, Michigan: Eerdmans, 1967. 47 pages.

Hardy, Evelyn. *Thomas Hardy: A Critical Biography.* New York: Russell and Russell, 1970. 342 pages.

Hartley, Lodwick, and George Core, eds. *Katherine Anne Porter: A Critical Symposium.* Athens, Georgia: University of Georgia Press, 1969. 242 pages.

Hatfield, Henry, ed. *Thomas Mann: A Collection of Critical Essays.* Englewood Cliffs, New Jersey: Prentice-Hall, 1964. 172 pages.

Heiney, Donald. *Simplified Approach to Hemingway.* Woodbury, New York: Barron's Educational Series, 1965. 120

pages.

Heiney, Donald. *Three Italian Novelists: Moravia, Pavese, Vittorini.* Ann Arbor: University of Michigan Press, 1968. 232 pages.

Heller, Erich. *Franz Kafka.* New York: Viking, 1975. 160 pages.

—. *Thomas Mann.* New York: P. P. Appel, 1973, c1958. 314 pages.

Hendin, Josephine. *The World of Flannery O'Connor.* Bloomington, Indiana: Indiana University Press, 1970. 177 pages.

Hersey, John, ed. *Ralph Ellison: A Collection of Critical Essays.* Englewood Cliffs, New Jersey: Prentice-Hall, 1969.

Hingley, Ronald. *Chekhov: A Biographical and Critical Study.* New York: Barnes and Noble, 1966. 256 pages.

Hoffman, Daniel G. *Poe Poe Poe Poe Poe Poe Poe.* New York: Doubleday, 1972. 339 pages.

Hoffman, Frederick J. *Conrad Aiken.* New York: Twayne, 1962. 172 pages.

—. *Gertrude Stein.* Minneapolis: University of Minnesota Press, 1973. 48 pages.

—. *Samuel Beckett: The Language of Self.* New York: E. P. Dutton, 1964. 177 pages.

Hoffman, Frederick J., and Olga W. Vickery, eds. *William Faulkner: Three Decades of Criticism.* New York: Harcourt Brace and World, 1963. 428 pages.

Hollingdale, R. J. *Thomas Mann: A Critical Study.* London: Hart-Davis, 1971. 204 pages.

Holloway, Jean. *Hamlin Garland.* Freeport, New York: Books for Libraries Press, 1971, c1960. 346 pages.

Holman, C. Hugh. *Thomas Wolfe.* Minneapolis: University of Minnesota Press, 1973. 47 pages.

Holmes, Charles, ed. *Thurber: A Collection of Critical Essays.* Englewood Cliffs, New Jersey: Prentice-Hall, 1974. 180 pages.

Holton, Milne. *Cylinders of Vision: The Fiction and Journalistic Writing of Stephen Crane.* Baton Rouge: Louisiana State University Press, 1972. 353 pages.

Howarth, William L., ed. *Twentieth-Century Interpretations of Poe's Tales: A Collection of Critical Essays.* Englewood Cliffs, New Jersey: Prentice-Hall, 1971. 116 pages.

Howe, Irving, ed. *Edith Wharton: A Collection of Critical Essays.* Englewood Cliffs, New Jersey: Prentice-Hall, 1962. 181 pages.

—. *Sherwood Anderson.* Stanford, California: Stanford University Press, 1966, c1951. 271 pages.

—. *Thomas Hardy.* London: Weidenfeld and Nicolson, 1968. 206 pages.

—. *William Faulkner: A Critical Study,* Second Edition. New York: Vintage, 1962. 299 pages.

Hynes, Samuel, ed. *Graham Greene: A Collection of Critical Essays.* Englewood Cliffs, New Jersey: Prentice-Hall, 1973. 183 pages.

Ignotus, Paul. *The Paradox of Maupassant.* New York: Funk and Wagnalls, 1968. 288 pages.

Ilie, Paul. *Unamuno: An Existential View of Self and Society.* Madison: University of Wisconsin Press, 1967. 299 pages.

Inge, M. Thomas, ed. *William Faulkner: "A Rose for Emily."* Columbus, Ohio: Charles E. Merrill, 1970.

Ireland, G. W. *André Gide: A Study of His Creative Writing.* New York: Oxford University Press, 1970. 448 pages.

Jackson, Robert Louis, ed. *Chekhov: A Collection of Critical Essays.* Englewood Cliffs, New Jersey: Prentice-Hall, 1967. 213 pages.

Jeffares, Alexander Norman, ed. *Scott's Mind and Art.* Edinburgh: Oliver and Boyd, 1969. 266 pages.

Johnson, Bruce. *Conrad's Modes of Mind.* Minneapolis: University of Minnesota Press, 1971. 48 pages.

Johnson, Ira. *Glenway Wescott: The Paradox of Voice.* Port Washington, New York: Kennikat Press, 1971. 209 pages.

Johnson, Pamela Hansford. *The Art of Thomas Wolfe.* New York: Scribner's, 1963. 170 pages.

Jordan, John Emory. *Thomas De Quincey, Literary Critic: His Method and Achievement.* Berkeley: University of California Press, 1952. 301 pages.

Joseph, Gerhard. *John Barth.* Minneapolis: University of Minnesota Press, 1970. 46 pages.

Josephson, Matthew. *Zola and His Time.* New York: Russell and Russell, 1969, c1928. 558 pages.

Karl, Frederick R. *A Reader's Guide to Joseph Conrad,* Rev. Ed. New York: Farrar, Straus and Giroux, 1969. 310 pages.

Katz, Joseph, ed. *Stephen Crane: "The Blue Hotel."* Columbus, Ohio: Charles E. Merrill, 1969.

—, ed. *Stephen Crane in Transition: Centenary Essays.* DeKalb: Northern Illinois University Press, 1971. 425 pages.

Kaul, A. N., ed. *Hawthorne: A Collection of Critical Essays.* Englewood Cliffs, New Jersey: Prentice-Hall, 1966. 182 pages.

Kazin, Alfred, ed. *F. Scott Fitzgerald: The Man and His Work.* New York: Collier Books, 1962, c1951. 221 pages.

Kelley, Cornelia. *The Early Development of Henry James.*

Urbana: University of Illinois Press, 1965. 319 pages.

Kenner, Hugh. *A Reader's Guide to Samuel Beckett.* London: Thames and Hudson, 1973. 208 pages.

Kern, Edith, ed. *Sartre: A Collection of Critical Essays.* Englewood Cliffs, New Jersey: Prentice-Hall, 1962. 179 pages.

Kieft, Ruth M. Vande. *Eudora Welty.* New York: Twayne, 1962. 203 pages.

Kinnamon, Kenneth. *The Emergence of Richard Wright.* Urbana, Illinois: University of Illinois Press, 1972. 200 pages.

—, ed. *James Baldwin: A Collection of Critical Essays.* Englewood Cliffs, New Jersey: Prentice-Hall, 1962. 179 pages.

Koch, Vivienne. *William Carlos Williams.* Norfolk, Connecticut: New Directions, 1950. 278 pages.

Korges, James. *Erskine Caldwell.* Minneapolis: University of Minnesota Press, 1969. 48 pages.

Kraft, James. *The Early Tales of Henry James.* Carbondale: Southern Illinois University Press, 1969. 143 pages.

Krutch, Joseph Wood. *Edgar Allan Poe: A Study of Genius.* New York: Russell and Russell, 1965, c1926. 244 pages.

Kuehn, Robert, ed. *Aldous Huxley: A Collection of Critical Essays.* Englewood Cliffs, New Jersey: Prentice-Hall, 1962. 188 pages.

Landess, Thomas H., ed. *The Short Fiction of Caroline Gordon: A Critical Symposium.* Dallas, Texas: University of Dallas Press, 1972.

Larsen, Erling. *James Agee.* Minneapolis: University of Minnesota Press, 1973. 48 pages.

Lary, N. M. *Dostoevsky and Dickens: A Study of Literary Influence.* London and Boston: Routledge and Kegan Paul, 1973. 172 pages.

Laser, Marvin, and Norman Fruman, eds. *Studies in J. D. Salinger.* New York: Odyssey Press, 1963. 272 pages.

Lavrin, Janko. *Nikolai Gogol.* New York: Russell and Russell, 1968. 174 pages.

—. *Pushkin and Russian Literature.* New York: Russell and Russell, 1969. 226 pages.

—. *Tolstoy: An Approach.* New York: Russell and Russell, 1968, c1946. 166 pages.

Lazere, Donald. *The Unique Creation of Albert Camus.* New Haven: Yale University Press, 1973. 271 pages.

Lehan, Richard D. *F. Scott Fitzgerald and the Craft of Fiction.* Carbondale: Southern Illinois University Press, 1966. 206 pages.

Levin, Dan. *Stormy Petrel: The Life and Work of Maxim Gorky.* New York: Appleton-Century, 1965. 332 pages.

Levin, Harry. *James Joyce: A Critical Introduction.* Norfolk, Connecticut: New Directions, 1960. 256 pages.

Levine, Stuart. *Edgar Allan Poe: Seer and Craftsman.* Deland, Florida: Everett/Edwards, 1972. 300 pages.

Lewis, Thomas S. W., ed. *Virginia Woolf: A Collection of Criticism.* New York: McGraw-Hill, 1975. 160 pages.

Liberman, M. M. *Katherine Anne Porter's Fiction.* Detroit: Wayne State University Press, 1971. 115 pages.

Littlejohn, David, ed. *Gide: A Collection of Critical Essays.* Englewood Cliffs, New Jersey: Prentice-Hall, 1970. 177 pages.

Litz, A. Walton. *The Art of James Joyce.* New York and London: Oxford University Press, 1961. 152 pages.

Lloyd, J. A. T. *Ivan Turgenev.* New York: Ryerson Press, 1942. 228 pages.

London, Charmian Kittredge. *The Book of Jack London*, 2 vols. London and New York: The Century Company, 1921.

Long, E. Hudson. *O. Henry: The Man and His Work.* New York: Russell and Russell, 1969, c1949. 158 pages.

Longley, John Lewis, ed. *Robert Penn Warren: A Collection of Critical Essays.* Englewood Cliffs, New Jersey: Prentice-Hall, 1965. 259 pages.

Lord, Robert. *Dostoevsky: Essays and Perspectives.* Berkeley: University of California Press, 1970. 254 pages.

Lucas, John. *Arnold Bennett: A Study of His Fiction.* New York: Barnes and Noble, 1975.

Lydenberg, John, ed. *Dreiser: A Collection of Critical Essays.* Englewood Cliffs, New Jersey: Prentice-Hall, 1971. 182 pages.

McDowell, Frederick P. W. *Caroline Gordon.* Minneapolis: University of Minnesota Press, 1966. 48 pages.

—. *E. M. Forster.* New York: Twayne, 173 pages.

Magalaner, Marvin. *The Fiction of Katherine Mansfield.* Carbondale: Southern Illinois University Presss, 1971. 148 pages.

Magarshack, David. *Chekhov: A Life.* London and New York: Oxford University Press, 1952 and 1953. 433 pages.

—. *Gogol: A Life.* New York: Grove Press, 1969. 328 pages.

Majumdar, Robin, and Allen McLaurin, eds. *Virginia Woolf: The Critical Heritage.* Boston and London: Routledge and Kegan Paul, 1975. 484 pages.

Malin, Irving, ed. *Critical Views of Isaac Bashevis Singer.* New York: New York University Press, 1969. 268 pages.

—, ed. *Saul Bellow and the Critics.* New York: New York University Press, 1967. 227 pages.

Maquet, Albert. *Albert Camus: The Invincible Summer.* New York: George Braziller, 1958. 224 pages.

Marchand, Ernest. *Frank Norris: A Study.* New York: Farrar, Straus and Giroux, reprint of 1942 edition. 258 pages.

Marder, Herbert. *Feminism and Art: A Study of Virginia Woolf.* Chicago: University of Chicago Press, 1968. 190 pages.

Margolies, Edward. *The Art of Richard Wright.* Carbondale: Southern Illinois University Press, 1969. 180 pages.

Marrot, Harold Vincent. *The Life and Letters of John Galsworthy.* London and New York: Scribner's, 1936. 819 pages.

Martin, Jay. *Conrad Aiken: A Life of His Art.* Princeton, New Jersey: Princeton University Press, 1962. 280 pages.

Matlaw, R. E., ed. *Tolstoy: A Collection of Critical Essays.* Englewood Cliffs, New Jersey: Prentice-Hall, 1967. 178 pages.

Matthiessen, F. O. *Henry James, the Major Phase.* New York: Oxford University Press, 1944. 190 pages.

—. *Sarah Orne Jewett.* Gloucester, Massachusetts: P. Smith, 1965, c1929. 159 pages.

—. *Theodore Dreiser.* Westport, Connecticut: Greenwich Press, reprint of 1951 edition. 267 pages.

Maurois, André. *Prometheus: The Life of Balzac.* London: Bodley Head, 1965. 573 pages.

Meckier, Jerome. *Aldous Huxley: Satire and Structure.* London: Chatto and Windus, 1969. 223 pages.

Migel, Parmenis. *Titania: The Biography of Isak Dinesen.* London: Joseph, 1968. 256 pages.

Miller, James E., Jr. *J. D. Salinger.* Minneapolis: University of Minnesota, 1973. 48 pages.

Miller, James E., Jr. *A Reader's Guide to Herman Melville.* New York: Farrar, Straus and Giroux, reprint of 1962 edition. 266 pages.

—. *Theory of Fiction: Henry James.* Lincoln: University of Nebraska Press, 1972. 366 pages.

Miller, J. Hillis. *Thomas Hardy: Distance and Desire.* Cambridge, Massachusetts: Harvard University Press, 1970. 282 pages.

—. *William Carlos Williams: A Collection of Critical Essays.* Englewood Cliffs, New Jersey: Prentice-Hall, 1966. 182 pages.

Mirsky, D. S. *Pushkin.* New York: E. P. Dutton and Company, 1973.

Mizener, Arthur, ed. *F. Scott Fitzgerald: A Collection of Critical Essays.* Englewood Cliffs, New Jersey: Prentice-Hall, 1963. 174 pages.

—. *The Far Side of Paradise* [about F. Scott Fitzgerald]. Boston: Houghton Mifflin, 1965. 416 pages.

—, *et al.,* eds. *Salinger.*

Mochulsky, Constantin. *Dostoyevsky: His Life and Work,* tr. Michael Minihan. Princeton, New Jersey: Princeton University Press, 1967. 687 pages.

Moore, Harry T. *D. H. Lawrence: His Life and Works,* Rev. Ed. New York: Twayne, 1964. 330 pages.

—. *John Steinbeck.* New York: Normandie House, 1939. 102 pages.

Moore, John R. *Daniel Defoe: Citizen of the Modern World.* Chicago: University of Chicago, 1958. 408 pages.

Morsberger, Robert E. *James Thurber.* New York: Twayne, 1964. 224 pages.

Moynihan, William. *The Craft and Art of Dylan Thomas.* Ithaca, New York: Cornell University Press, 1966. 304 pages.

Mudrick, Marvin, ed. *Conrad: A Collection of Critical Essays.* Englewood Cliffs, New Jersey: Prentice-Hall, 1966. 182 pages.

Muller, Gilbert H. *Nightmare and Vision: Flannery O'Connor and the Catholic Grotesque.* Athens: University of Georgia Press, 1972. 121 pages.

Myers, Andrew B., ed. *Washington Irving: A Tribute.* Sleepy Hollow Press, 1975.

Nabokov, Vladimir. *Nikolai Gogol.* Norfolk, Connecticut: New Directions, 1944. 172 pages.

Nahal, Chaman. *The Narrative Pattern in Ernest Hemingway's Fiction.* Rutherford, New Jersey: Fairleigh Dickinson University Press, 1971. 245 pages.

Nance, William L. *The Worlds of Truman Capote.* New York: Stein and Day, 1970. 256 pages.

Neider, Charles. *The Frozen Sea: A Study of Franz Kakfa.* Toronto: Oxford University Press, 1948. 195 pages.

—, ed. *The Stature of Thomas Mann: A Critical Anthology.* New York: New Directions, 1947. 510 pages.

Nevius, Blake. *Edith Wharton: A Study of Her Fiction.* Berkeley: University of California Press, 1953. 271 pages.

New York Times Editors. *John Updike: The Author and His Work.* New York: Fawcett, 1975.

Norman, Frederick, ed. *Hoffmensthal: Studies in Commemoration.* London: University of London, 1963.

O'Brien, Justin. *Portrait of André Gide: A Critical Biography.* New York: Farrar, Straus and Giroux, 1953. 390 pages.

O'Connor, Richard. *Ambrose Bierce.* Boston: Little, Brown,

1967. 333 pages.

O'Connor, Richard. *Jack London: A Biography.* Boston: Little, Brown, 1964. 430 pages.

O'Connor, William Van. *The Tangled Fire of William Faulkner.* New York: Gordimer Press, 1968, c1954. 182 pages.

Ohlin, Peter H. *Agee.* Ann Arbor, Michigan: University of Michigan, 1965. 316 pages.

Orvell, Miles. *Invisible Parade: The Fiction of Flannery O'Connor.* Philadelphia: Temple University Press, 1972. 249 pages.

Owens, Graham, ed. *George Moore's Mind and Art.* New York: Barnes and Noble, 1970, c1968. 182 pages.

Painter, George D. *André Gide: A Critical Biography.* London: Weidenfeld and Nicolson, 1968. 148 pages.

Parker, Emmett. *Albert Camus: The Artist in the Arena.* Madison: University of Wisconsin Press, 1965. 245 pages.

Parrinder, Patrick, ed. *H. G. Wells: The Critical Heritage.* Boston: Routledge and Kegan Paul, 1972. 351 pages.

Patrick, Walton R. *Ring Lardner.* New York: Twayne, 1963. 175 pages.

Pearce, T. M. *Oliver La Farge.* New York: Twayne, 1972. 152 pages.

Piper, Henry Dan. *F. Scott Fitzgerald.* London: Feffer and Simons, Inc., 1965. 334 pages.

Powers, Lyall H. *Henry James and the Naturalist Movement.* East Lansing, Michigan: Michigan State University Press, 1971. 200 pages.

Pratt, Annis. *Dylan Thomas' Early Prose: A Study in Creative Mythology.* Pittsburgh: University of Pittsburgh Press, 1970. 226 pages.

Putt, S. Gorley. *Henry James: A Reader's Guide.* Ithaca, New York: Cornell University Press, 1966. 432 pages.

Quinn, Arthur Hobson. *Edgar Allan Poe: A Critical Biography.* New York: Cooper Square, 1969, c1941. 804 pages.

Quinn, Patrick F. *Poe and France: The Last Twenty Years.* Baltimore: Edgar Allan Poe Society, 1970. 22 pages.

Quintana, Ricardo. *Oliver Goldsmith: A Georgian Study.* New York: Macmillan, 1967. 213 pages.

Rankin, Daniel S. *Kate Chopin and Her Creole Stories.* Philadelphia: University of Pennsylvania Press, 1932. 339 pages.

Ratner, Marc L. *William Styron.* New York: Twayne, 1972. 170 pages.

Reed, Joseph W. *Faulkner's Narrative.* New Haven: Yale University Press, 1973. 303 pages.

Regan, Robert, ed. *Poe: A Collection of Critical Essays.* Englewood Cliffs, New Jersey: Prentice-Hall, 1967. 183 pages.

Reichert, Herbert W., and Herman Salinger, eds. *Studies in Arthur Schnitzler.* Chapel Hill, North Carolina: University of North Carolina Press, 1963. 116 pages.

Reilly, J., ed. *Twentieth-Century Interpretations of [Ralph Ellison's] Invisible Man.* Englewood Cliffs, New Jersey: Prentice-Hall, 1970. 120 pages.

Richman, Sidney. *Bernard Malamud.* New York: Twayne, 1967, c1966. 160 pages.

Richter, Harvena. *Virginia Woolf: The Inward Voyage.* Princeton: Princeton University Press, 1970. 273 pages.

Rideout, Walter B., ed. *Sherwood Anderson: A Collection of Critical Essays.* Englewood Cliffs, New Jersey: Prentice-Hall, 1974. 177 pages.

Robinson, Michael. *The Long Sonata of the Dead: A Study of*

Samuel Beckett.   New York: Grove Press, 1970, c1969. 318 pages.

Rogers, Pat, ed. *Defoe: The Critical Heritage.* Boston and London: Routledge and Kegan Paul, 1972. 228 pages.

Rohrberger, Mary. *Hawthorne and the Modern Short Story: A Study in Genre.* The Hague: Mouton, 1966. 148 pages.

Ross, Joan, and Donald Freed. *The Existentialism of Albert Moravia.* Carbondale: Southern Illinois University, 1972. 172 pages.

Rousseau, G. S., ed. *Goldsmith: The Critical Heritage.* Boston and London: Routledge and Kegan Paul, 1975.

Roussel, Royal. *The Metaphysics of Darkness: A Study in the Unity and Development of Conrad's Fiction.* Baltimore: Johns Hopkins Press, 1971. 194 pages.

Rovit, Earl. *Saul Bellow.* Minneapolis: University of Minnesota Press, 1967. 46 pages.

—, ed. *Saul Bellow: A Collection of Critical Essays.* Englewood Cliffs, New Jersey: Prentice-Hall, 1975.

Rowe, William W. *Nabokov's Deceptive World.* New York: New York University Press, 1971. 193 pages.

Rubin, Louis D., Jr. *George W. Cable: The Life and Times of a Southern Heretic.* New York: Pegasus, 1969. 304 pages.

—. *Thomas Wolfe: The Weather of His Youth.* Baton Rouge: Louisiana State University Press, 1955. 183 pages.

Rutherford, Andrew, ed. *Kipling's Mind and Art: Selected Critical Essays.* Stanford, California: Stanford University Press, 1964. 278 pages.

Rysten, Felix S. A. *False Prophets in the Fiction of Camus, Dostoevsky, Melville, and Others.* Coral Gables, Florida: University of Miami Press, 1972. 139 pages.

Sachs, Murray. *The Career of Alphonse Daudet: A Critical Study.* Cambridge, Massachusetts: Harvard University Press, 1965. 227 pages.

Sackville-West, Edward. *A Flame in Sunlight* [about Thomas De Quincey]. New Haven: Yale University Press, 1940.

Samuel, Maurice. *Prince of the Ghetto* [about Isaac Loeb Peretz]. New York: A. A. Knopf, 1963. 294 pages.

—. *The World of Sholom Aleichem.* New York: Random House, 1965. 331 pages.

Samuels, Charles Thomas. *The Ambiguity of Henry James.* Urbana, Illinois: University of Illinois Press, 1971.

—. *John Updike.* Minneapolis: University of Minnesota Press, 1969. 46 pages.

Scheer-Schäzler, Brigitte. *Saul Bellow.* New York: Ungar, 1972. 150 pages.

Schevill, James Erwin. *Sherwood Anderson: His Life and Work.* Denver: University of Denver, 1951. 390 pages.

Schmitter, Dean M., ed. *William Faulkner: A Collection of Criticism.* New York: McGraw-Hill, 1973. 153 pages.

Scholes, Robert, and A. Walton Litz, eds. *Dubliners: Text, Criticism, and Notes.* New York: Viking, 1969. 504 pages.

Schorer, Mark. *Sinclair Lewis: An American Life.* New York: McGraw-Hill, 1961. 867 pages.

—, ed. *Sinclair Lewis: A Collection of Critical Essays.* Englewood Cliffs, New Jersey: Prentice-Hall, 1962. 174 pages.

Schwarzschild, Bettina. *The Not-Right House: Essays on James Purdy.* Columbia: University of Missouri Press, 1968. 65 pages.

Scott, Arthur L., ed. *Mark Twain: Selected Criticism.* Dallas: Southern Methodist University Press, 1967. 306 pages.

Segal, Ora. *The Lucid Reflector: The Observer in Henry James' Fiction.* New Haven: Yale University Press, 1969. 265 pages.

Sergeant, Elizabeth Shepley. *Willa Cather: A Memoir.* Lincoln: University of Nebraska Press, 1963. 303 pages.

Setchkarev, Vsevolod. *Gogol: His Life and Works,* tr. R. Kramer. New York: New York University Press, 1965. 264 pages.

Sheehy, Maurice, ed. *Michael/Frank: Studies in Frank O'Connor.* New York: A. A. Knopf, 1969. 203 pages.

Sherry, Norman, ed. *Conrad: The Critical Heritage.* Boston and London: Routledge and Kegan Paul, 1973. 393 pages.

Siegel, Ben. *Isaac Bashevis Singer.* Minneapolis: University of Minnesota Press, 1969. 48 pages.

Simmons, Ernest J. *Chekhov: A Biography.* Chicago: University of Chicago Press, 1970. 630 pages.

—. *Introduction to Tolstoy's Writings.* Chicago: University of Chicago Press, 1968. 220 pages.

—. *Tolstoy.* Boston and London: Routledge and Kegan Paul, 1975.

Sitz, Walter. *Heinrich Von Kleist: Studies in His Works and Literary Character.* Philadelphia and Oxford: Oxford University Press, 1962.

Sklar, Robert A. *F. Scott Fitzgerald, the Last Laocoön.* London and New York: Oxford University Press, 1967. 376 pages.

Slote, Bernice, and Virginia Faulkner, eds. *The Art of Willa Cather.* Lincoln: University of Nebraska Press, 1975. 225 pages.

Smith, Henry Nash, ed. *Mark Twain: A Collection of Critical Essays.* Englewood Cliffs, New Jersey: Prentice-Hall, 1963.

179 pages.

Solomon, Eric. *Stephen Crane: From Parody to Realism.* Cambridge, Massachusetts: Harvard University Press, 1966. 301 pages.

Speirs, Logan. *Tolstoy and Chekhov.* Cambridge, England: Cambridge University Press, 1971. 237 pages.

Spilka, Mark. *The Love Ethic of D. H. Lawrence.* Bloomington, Indiana: Indiana University Press, 1955. 244 pages.

Sprague, Claire, ed. *Virginia Woolf: A Collection of Critical Essays.* Englewood Cliffs, New Jersey: Prentice-Hall, 1971. 185 pages.

Sprigge, Elizabeth. *Gertrude Stein: Her Life and Work.* New York: Harper, 1957. 277 pages.

Stabb, Martin S. *Jorge Luis Borges.* New York: Twayne, 1970. 179 pages.

Stallman, R. W. *Stephen Crane: A Biography.* New York: George Braziller, 1968. 664 pages.

Stanford, Derek. *Dylan Thomas: A Literary Study.* New York: Citadel Press, 1965, c1964. 212 pages.

Starkie, Enid. *Baudelaire.* London: Faber and Faber, 1957. 662 pages.

—. *Flaubert: The Making of the Master.* New York: Atheneum, 1967. 403 pages.

Starkie, Walter. *Luigi Pirandello,* 3rd Ed., revised and enlarged. Berkeley: Univeristy of California Press, 1965. 304 pages.

Steegmuller, Francis. *Maupassant: A Lion in the Path.* New York: Random House, 1949. 430 pages.

Stein, Gertrude. *The Autobiography of Alice B. Toklas.* New York: Random House, 1933. 310 pages.

Stewart, George R. *Bret Harte: Argonaut and Exile.* Boston and New York: Houghton Mifflin, 1931. 385 pages.

Stewart, J. I. M. *Rudyard Kipling.* New York: Dodd, Mead, 1966. 245 pages.

Stock, Irvin. *Mary McCarthy.* Minneapolis: University of Minnesota Press, 1973. 48 pages.

Stone, Wilfred. *The Cave and the Mountain: A Study of E. M. Forster.* Stanford, California: Stanford University Press, 1966. 436 pages.

Stouck, David. *Willa Cather's Imagination.* Lincoln: University of Nebraska Press, 1975. 240 pages.

Stuckey, W. J. *Caroline Gordon.* New York: Twayne, 1972. 188 pages.

Sutherland, Donald. *Gertrude Stein: A Biography of Her Work.* Westport, Connecticut: Greenwood Press, reprint of 1951 edition. 218 pages.

Sutherland, James R. *Defoe.* London, 1950.

Swanberg, William A. *Dreiser.* New York: Scribner's, 1965. 614 pages.

Szanto, George Herbert. *Narrative Consciousness: Structure and Perception in the Fiction of Kafka, Beckett, and Robbe-Grillet.* Austin: University of Texas Press, 1972. 216 pages.

Tauber, Herbert. *Franz Kafka: An Interpretation of His Works.* New York: Haskell House Publishers, 1967. 252 pages.

Taylor, Larrey E. *Pastoral and Anti-Pastoral Patterns in John Updike's Fiction.* Carbondale: Southern Illinois University Press, 1971. 159 pages.

Tedlock, E. W., Jr. *D. H. Lawrence, Artist and Rebel: A Study of Lawrence's Fiction.* Albuquerque: University of New Mexico Press, 1963. 242 pages.

Thody, Philip. *Albert Camus.* London: H. Hamilton, 1961. 242 pages.

—. *Huxley: A Biographical Introduction.* New York: Scribner's, 1973. 144 pages.

Thompson, G. R. *Poe's Fiction: Romantic Irony in the Gothic Tales.* Madison: University of Wisconsin Press, 1973. 272 pages.

Thompson, Lawrance Roger. *William Faulkner: An Introduction and an Interpretation.* New York: Barnes and Noble, 1963. 184 pages.

Thorp, Margaret F. *Sarah Orne Jewett.* Minneapolis: University of Minnesota Press, 1966. 48 pages.

Thorpe, Michael. *Doris Lessing.* Harlow, England: Longman Group, 1973. 37 pages.

Tindall, William York. *A Reader's Guide to Dylan Thomas.* New York: Farrar, Straus and Groux, reprint of 1962 edition. 320 pages.

—. *A Reader's Guide to James Joyce.* New York: Farrar, Straus and Giroux, reprint of 1959 edition. 304 pages.

Tobias, Richard C. *The Art of James Thurber.* Athens, Ohio: Ohio University Press, 1969. 196 pages.

Tompkins, Jane P., ed. *Twentieth-Century Interpretations of "The Turn of the Screw" and Other Tales.* Englewood Cliffs, New Jersey: Prentice-Hall, 1970. 115 pages.

Trilling, Lionel. *E. M. Forster,* 2nd rev. ed. New York: New Directions, 1965, c1964, c1944. 194 pages.

Trimmer, Joseph F., ed. *A Casebook on Ralph Ellison's Invisible Man.* New York: Crowell, 1972. 312 pages.

Tuckey, John S. *Mark Twain and Little Satan.* West Lafayette, Indiana: Purdue University Studies, 1963. 101 pages.

Turnbull, Andrew. *Scott Fitzgerald.* New York: Scribner's, 1963. 360 pages.

Turnell, Martin. *Baudelaire.* Norfolk, Connecticut: New Directions, 1954. 328 pages.

Turner, Arlin. *George W. Cable: A Biography.* Durham, North Carolina: Duke University Press, 1956. 391 pages.

Tylden-Wright, David. *Anatole France.* New York: Walker, 1967. 344 pages.

Utley, Francis Lee, Lynn Z. Bloom, and Arthur F. Kinney, eds. *Bear, Man, and God: Eight Approaches to William Faulkner's "The Bear,"* 2nd ed. New York: Random House, 1971. 336 pages.

Vaid, K. B. *Technique in the Tales of Henry James.* Cambridge, Massachusetts: Harvard University Press, 1964. 285 pages.

Volpe, Edmond L. *A Reader's Guide to William Faulkner.* New York: Farrar, Starus and Giroux, reprint of 1964 edition. 427 pages.

Von Gronicka, André. *Thomas Mann: Profile and Perspectives.* New York: Random House, 1973.

Wagenknecht, Edward. *Washington Irving: Moderation Displayed.* New York: Oxford University Press, 1962. 223 pages.

—. *Edgar Allan Poe: The Man Behind the Legend.* New York: Oxford University Press, 1963. 276 pages.

Waggoner, Hyatt H. *Hawthorne: A Critical Study.* Cambridge, Massachusetts: Harvard University Press, 1955. 268 pages.

Waife-Goldberg, Marie. *My Father, Sholom Aleichem.* New York: Simon and Schuster, 1968. 333 pages.

Wain, John. *Arnold Bennett.* New York: Columbia University Press, 1967. 47 pages.

Walcutt, Charles Child. *Jack London.* Minneapolis: University of Minnesota Press, 1966. 48 pages.

Waldhorn, Arthur. *Ernest Hemingway,* ed. Eugene Ehrlich and Daniel Murphy. New York: McGraw-Hill, 1972. 160 pages.

—. *A Reader's Guide to Ernest Hemingway.* New York: Noonday Press, 1972. 284 pages.

Walsh, J. *Poe the Detective: The Curious Circumstances Behind the Mystery of Marie Roget.* New Brunswick, New Jersey: Rutgers University Press, 1968. 154 pages.

Warren, Robert Penn, ed. *Faulkner: A Collection of Critical Essays.* Englewood Cliffs, New Jersey: Prentice-Hall, 1966. 311 pages.

Watt, Donald, ed. *Aldous Huxley: The Critical Heritage.* Boston: Routledge and Kegan Paul, 1975. 517 pages.

Weatherford, Richard M., ed. *Stephen Crane: The Critical Heritage.* Boston: Routledge and Kegan Paul, 1973. 343 pages.

Weathers, Winston. *Pär Lagerkvist.* Grand Rapids, Michigan: Eerdmans, 1968. 47 pages.

Weber, Brom. *Sherwood Anderson.* Minneapolis: University of Minnesota Press, 1964. 48 pages.

Weber, Carl J. *Hardy of Wessex: His Life and Literary Career,* rev. ed. New York: Columbia University Press, 1965, c1940. 324 pages.

Weeks, Robert P., ed. *Hemingway: A Collection of Critical Essays.* Englewood Cliffs, New Jersey: Prentice-Hall, 1962. 180 pages.

Weil, Irwin. *Gorky: His Literary Development and Influence on Soviet Intellectual Life.* New York: Random House, 1966. 238 pages.

Wellek, René, ed. *Dostoevsky: A Collection of Critical Essays.* Englewood Cliffs, New Jersey: Prentice-Hall, 1962. 180 pages.

West, Paul. *Robert Penn Warren.* Minneapolis: University of Minnesota Press, 1964. 48 pages.

West, Ray B., Jr. *Katherine Anne Porter.* Minneapolis: University of Minnesota Press, 1963. 48 pages.

Westbrook, Max. *Walter Van Tilburg Clark.* New York: Twayne, 1969. 166 pages.

Westbrook, Perry D. *Mary Ellen Chase.* New York: Twayne, 1965. 176 pages.

Wexford, Jane. *Monarch Literature Notes on Chekhov's Plays and Stories.* Monarch, 1974.

Whissen, Thomas R. *Isak Dinesen's Aesthetics.* Kennikat Press, 1974.

Widmer, Kingsley. *The Ways of Nihilism: A Study of Melville's Short Novels.* Los Angeles: California State Colleges Press, 1970. 149 pages.

Wiggins, Lida Keck. *The Life and Works of Paul Laurence Dunbar.* New York: Nichols, 1907. n.p.

Wilde, Alan. *Art and Order: A Study of E. M. Forster.* New York: New York University Press, 1964. 179 pages.

Winner, Thomas. *Chekhov and His Prose.* New York: Holt, Rinehart and Winston, 1966. 263 pages.

Woodress, James. *Booth Tarkington, Gentleman from Indiana.* Westport, Connecticut: Greenwood Press, reprint of 1955 edition. '350 pages.

—. *Willa Cather: Her Life and Art.* Lincoln: University of Nebraska Press, 1975. 288 pages.

Worth, Katharine, ed. *Beckett the Shape Changer.* Boston and

London: Routledge and Kegan Paul, 1975. 238 pages.

Wylder, Delbert E. *Hemingway's Heroes.* Albuquerque: University of New Mexico Press, 1969. 255 pages.

Yarmolinsky, Avrahm. *Dostoyevsky: His Life and Art,* 2nd ed., revised and enlarged. New York: Criterion Books, 1957. 434 pages.

—. *Turgenev: The Man, His Art, and His Age.* New York: Orion Press, 1959. 406 pages.

Young, Philip. *Ernest Hemingway.* Minneapolis: University of Minnesota Press, 1966, c1964. 48 pages.

III. COLLECTIONS AND ANTHOLOGIES OF THE SHORT STORY, MORE THAN ONE AUTHOR

Abrahams, William, ed. *Fifty Years of the American Short Story from the O. Henry Awards 1919-1970*, vols. 1-2. Garden City, New York: Doubleday, 1970.

—. *Prize Stories 1971: The O. Henry Awards.* Garden City, New York: Doubleday, 1971.

Albrecht, Robert C., ed. *The World of Short Fiction.* New York: Free Press, 1969. 580 pages.

Allen, Dick, and David Chocko. *Detective Fiction.* Harcourt Brace Jovanovich, 1974. 481 pages.

Allen, Dick, and Lori Allen. *Looking Ahead: The Vision of Science Fiction.* Harcourt Brace Jovanovich, 1974. 408 pages.

Allen, Donald M., and Robert Creeley. *New American Story.* New York: Grove Press, 1968. 278 pages.

Aloian, David, ed. *Stories and Storytellers.* Menlo Park, California: Addison-Wesley Publishing, 1968. 273 pages.

Altenbernd, Lynn, and Leslie L. Lewis, eds. *Introduction to Literature: Stories,* 2nd ed. New York: Macmillan, 1969. 491 pages.

Alvarez, A., ed. *Hungarian Short Stories.* New York: Oxford University Press, 1967. 432 pages.

Alwin, Virginia, ed. *Currents in Fiction,* rev. ed. New York: Macmillan, 1968. 301 pages.

Angoff, Charles, ed. *Modern Stories from Many Lands.* New York: Manyland Books, 1972.

—. *Stories from the Literary Review.* Rutherford, New Jersey: Fairleigh Dickinson University Press, 1969. 312 pages.

Angus, Douglas, ed. *The Best Short Stories of the Modern Age.* Greenwich, Connecticut: Fawcett, 1962. 334 pages.

—, and Sylvia Angus, eds. *Contemporary American Short Stories.* Greenwich, Connecticut: Fawcett, 1967. 448 pages.

—. *Great Modern European Short Stories.* Greenwich, Connecticut: Fawcett, 1967. 383 pages.

—. *Love Is the Theme.* Greenwich, Connecticut: Fawcett, 1970. 334 pages.

Angus, Sylvia, ed. *The Trouble Is: Stories of Social Dilemma.* Encino, California: Dickenson Publishing Company, 1973. 433 pages.

Ashley, Leonard R., and Stuart L. Astor, eds. *British Short Stories: Classics and Criticism.* Englewood Cliffs, New Jersey: Prentice-Hall, 1968. 417 pages.

Ashley, Leonard. *Other People's Lives: Thirty-Four Short Stories.* Boston: Houghton Mifflin, 1970. 418 pages.

Bach, Bert C., and Gordon Browning, eds. *Fiction for Composition.* Glenview, Illinois: Scott, Foresman, 1968. 388 pages.

Ball, Jane Eklund, ed. *Design for Reading: Short Stories.* Boston: Houghton Mifflin, 1969. 250 pages.

—. *Range of Literature: Fiction.* Boston: Houghton Mifflin, 1973.

Barroll, John Leeds, III, and Austin M. Wright. *The Art of the Short Story: An Introductory Anthology.* Boston: Allyn and Bacon, 1969. 479 pages.

Barrows, Herbert, ed. *An Introduction to Literature: Reading the Short Story.* Boston: Houghton Mifflin, 1959. 338 pages.

Bates, H. E. *The Modern Short Story: A Critical Survey.* Boston: The Writer, Inc., 1972. 231 pages.

Baudin, Maurice, Jr., ed. *Contemporary Short Stories,* 3 vols. Indianapolis: Bobbs-Merrill, 1953-1954.

—, ed. *Edgar Allan Poe and Others: Representative Short Stories of the Nineteenth Century.* New York: Liberal Arts Press, 1953, c1952. 117 pages.

Baumbach, Jonathan, and Arthur Edelstein, eds. *Moderns and Contemporaries: Nine Masters of the Short Story.* New York: Random House, 1968. 422 pages.

Bearne, C. G., ed. *Modern Russian Short Stories.* London: Mac-Gibbon and Kee, 1968. vol, n.p.

—, ed. *Vortex: New Soviet Science Fiction.* London: Mac-Gibbon and Kee, 1970. 224 pages.

Beaty, Jerome, ed. *Fiction.* New York: W. W. Norton and Company, 1973. 613 pages.

Becker, May, ed. *Golden Tales of Canada.* Freeport, New York: Books for Libraries Press, 1972 reprint of 1938 edition. 274 pages.

Beier, Ulli, ed. *Black Orpheus: An Anthology of African and Afro-American Prose.* London: Longmans, 1964.

Beja, Morris. *Psychological Fiction.* Glenview, Illinois: Scott, Foresman, 1971. 499 pages.

Bellow, Saul, ed. *Great Jewish Short Stories.* London: Vallentine, Mitchell, 1971. 414 pages.

Benedict, Stewart, ed. *The Crime-Solvers: 13 Classic Detective Stories.* New York: Dell, 1975.

Benedict, Stewart, ed. *Tales of Terror and Suspense.* New York: Dell, 1975.

Benjamin, Lewis S., and Reginald Hargreaves, eds. *Great German Short Stories.* Freeport, New York: Books for Libraries Press, 1971 reprint of 1929 edition. 1012 pages.

Bennett, George, ed. *Great Tales of Action and Adventure.* New York: Dell, 1965, c1959. 256 pages.

Berdan, John Milton, ed. *Fourteen Stories from One Plot* (based on "Mr. Fothergill's Plot"). Freeport, New York: Books for Libraries Press, 1971 reprint of 1932 edition. 287 pages.

Bergin, Thomas G., ed. *Modern Italian Short Stories.* Boston: Heath, 1959. 225 pages.

Berner, Heinz, ed. *English Short Stories of the Nineteenth Century.* Hildesheim, New York: G. Olms, 1969. 486 pages.

Berkley, Saudra Gould, ed. *The Short Story Reader,* 3rd ed. Indianapolis: Odyssey Press, 1973. 495 pages.

Bierman, Judah, James Hart, and Stanley Johnson, eds. *Discovery and Response: The Strategies of Fiction.* Englewood Cliffs, New Jersey: Prentice-Hall (Winthrop), 1972. 483 pages.

Blair, Thomas, ed. *Fifty Modern Stories.* Evanston, Illinois: Row, Peterson, 1960. 723 pages.

Bloom, Edward Alan, ed. *The Order of Fiction: An Introduction.* New York: Odyssey, 1964. 246 pages.

—, and Lilliam D. Bloom, eds. *The Variety of Fiction: A Critical Anthology.* New York: Odyssey, 1969. 464 pages.

Bonazza, Blaze Odell, and Emil Roy, eds. *Studies in Fiction.* New York: Harper-Row, 1965. 384 pages.

Booth, Michael R., and Clinton L. Burhans, Jr., eds. *Thirty-One Stories.* Engewood Cliffs, New Jersey: Prentice-Hall,

1960. 364 pages.

Bowen, James K., and Richard VanDerBeets, eds. *American Short Fiction: Readings and Criticism.* Indianapolis: Bobbs-Merrill, 1970. 454 pages.

—. *Classic Short Fiction: An International Collection.* Indianapolis: Bobbs-Merrill, 1972. 526 pages.

Boynton, Robert W., and Maynard Mack, eds. *Introduction to the Short Story.* Rochelle Park, New Jersey: Hayden Book Company, 1972. 304 pages.

Brée, Germaine, ed. *Great French Short Stories.* New York: Dell, 1974.

Brewster, Dorothy, ed. *A Book of Contemporary Short Stories.* New York: Macmillan, 1936. 754 pages.

—, ed. *A Book of Modern Short Stories.* New York: Macmillan, 1928. 482 pages.

—, and Angus Burrell, eds. *Modern Fiction.* New York: Columbia University Press, 1934. 442 pages.

Brickell, Herschel, and Muriel Fuller, eds. *O. Henry Memorial Award Prize Stories of 1943-1948.* Garden City, New York: Doubleday, 1943-1948.

Brissenden, R. F., ed. *Southern Harvest: An Anthology of Australian Short Stories.* New York: St. Martin's Press, 1965, c1964. 288 pages.

Brooks, Cleanth, and Robert Penn Warren, eds. *The Scope of Fiction.* New York: Appleton-Century-Crofts, 1960. 336 pages.

—, eds. *Understanding Fiction,* 2nd ed. New York: Appleton-Century-Crofts, 1959. 688 pages.

Brotherston, G., and M. V. Llosa, eds. *Seven Stories from Spanish America.* Oxford, New York: Pergamon Press, 1968.

98 pages.

Brown, Leonard Stanley, ed. *Stories from the Quarto.* New York: Scribner's, 1968. 179 pages.

Buckler, William Earl, and Arnold B. Sklare, eds. *Stories from Six Authors,* First Series. New York: McGraw-Hill, 1960. 512 pages.

—, eds. *Stories from Six Authors,* Second Series. New York: McGraw-Hill, 1966. 417 pages.

Burnett, Whit. *The Maker of Signs: A Variety.* Freeport, New York: Books for Libraries Press, 1970 reprint of 1934 edition. 320 pages.

Burrell, John A., and Bennett Cerf, eds. *An Anthology of Famous American Stories.* New York: Modern Library, 1953. 1340 pages.

Cahill, Tom and Susan, eds. *Big City Stories by Modern American Writers.* New York: Bantam, 1971. 405 pages.

Calderwood, James L., and Harold E. Toliver, eds. *Forms of Prose Fiction.* Englewood Cliffs, New Jersey: Prentice-Hall, 1972. 482 pages.

Callaghan, Morley, ed. *A Native Argosy.* Freeport, New York: Books for Libraries Press, 1970 reprint of 1929 edition. 371 pages.

Canby, Henry Seidel, and Robeson Bailey, eds. *The Book of the Short Story,* new and enlarged edition. New York: Appleton-Century-Crofts, 1948. n.p.

Canzoneri, Robert, and Page Stegner, eds. *Fiction and Analysis: Seven Major Themes.* Glenview, Illinois: Scott, Foresman, 1970. 452 pages.

Carey, Glen O., ed. *Quest for Meaning: Modern Short Stories.* New York: David McKay, 1975. 320 pages.

Carson, Herbert L., and Ada Lou Carson, eds. *The Impact of*

Fiction: An Anthology of Short Stories. Glenview, Illinois: Scott, Foresman, 1970. 452 pages.

Casty, Alan, ed. *The Shape of Fiction: Stories for Comparison.* Boston: D. C. Heath, 1967. 400 pages.

Cerf, Bennett, and Henry C. Moriarty, eds. *The Bedside Book of British Stories.* New York: Random House, 1966, c1940. 1233 pages.

Cerf, Bennett, ed. *Famous Ghost Stories.* New York: Random House, 1966. 361 pages.

—, ed. *Great Modern Short Stories.* New York: Random House, 1966. 456 pages.

—, ed. *Modern American Short Stories.* New York: Random House, 1945. 384 pages.

—, ed. *Stories to Make You Feel Better.* New York: Random House, 1972. 109 pages.

Charles, Gerda, ed. *Modern Jewish Stories.* Englewood Cliffs, New Jersey: Prentice-Hall, 1965, c1963. 276 pages.

Charyn, Jerome, ed. *The Single Voice: An Anthology of Contemporary Fiction.* New York: Collier Books, 1969. 516 pages.

—, ed. *The Troubled Vision: An Anthology of Contemporary Short Stories.* New York: Collier Books, 1970. 510 pages.

Clarke, John Henrik, ed. *American Negro Short Stories.* New York: Hill and Wang, 1966. 355 pages.

Cline, Clarence Lee, ed. *The Rinehart Book of Short Stories.* New York: Holt, Rinehart, and Winston, 1964. 307 pages.

Coan, Otis W., and Richard Lillard, eds. *America in Fiction.* Stanford, California: Stanford University Press, 1945. 162 pages.

Cody, Sherwin, ed. *Selection from the World's Greatest Short Stories.* Freeport, New York: Books for Libraries Press, 1970 reprint of 1902 edition. 412 pages.

Colford, William Edward, tr. and ed. *Classic Tales from Modern Spain.* Great Neck, New York: Barron's Educational Series, 1964. 201 pages.

—, ed. *Classic Tales from Spanish America.* Great Neck, New York: Barron's Educational Series, 1962. 210 pages.

Cooper, Burton L., and Lila K. Chalpin, eds. *Achievements in Fiction: A College Anthology.* Boston: Allyn and Bacon, 1971. 538 pages.

Corder, Jim W., ed. *Finding a Voice.* Glenview, Illinois: Scott, Foresman, 1973. 796 pages.

Costain, Thomas B., and John Beecroft, eds. *More Stories to Remember.* Garden City, New York: Doubleday, 1958. 2 vols.

Costain, Thomas B., ed. *Read With Me.* Garden City, New York: Doubleday, 1965. 623 pages.

Costain, Thomas B., and John Beecroft, eds. *Stories to Remember.* Garden City, New York: Doubleday, 1956. 2 vols.

—, eds. *Thirty Stories to Remember.* Garden City, New York: Doubleday, 1962. 884 pages.

Coulos, James, ed. *Youth and Maturity: Twenty Short Stories.* New York: Macmillan, 1970. 376 pages.

Coulson, Jessie, and Natalie Duddington, eds. *Russian Short Stories: Nineteenth Century.* Oxford: Clarendon Press, 1953. 240 pages.

Cournos, John, ed. *American Short Stories of the Nineteenth Century.* New York: E. P. Dutton and Company, Inc., 1960. 372 pages.

Cowan, Gregory, *et al*, eds. *Three for Show: A Visual Approach to the Short Story.* New York: Random House, 1973. 156 pages.

Crane, Milton, ed. *Fifty Great American Short Stories.* New York: Bantam, 1965. 502 pages.

—. *Fifty Great Short Stories.* New York: Bantam, 1952. 632 pages.

Cross, Ethan Allen, ed. *A Book of the Short Story.* New York: American Book Company, 1934. 1103 pages.

Current-Garcia, Eugene and Walton R. Patrick, eds. *American Short Stories,* third edition. Glenview, Illinois: Scott, Foresman, 1976. 688 pages.

—, eds. *Realism and Romanticism in Fiction.* Chicago: Scott, Foresman, 1962. 504 pages.

—, eds. *Short Stories of the Western World.* Glenview, Illinois: Scott, Foresman, 1969. 653 pages.

—, eds. *What Is the Short Story?,* revised edition. Glenview, Illinois: Scott, Foresman, 1974. 532 pages.

Dalziel, Margaret, ed. *Popular Fiction 100 Years Ago.* London: Cohen and West, 1957. 188 pages.

Davis, Beatrice, ed. *Short Stories of Australia: The Moderns.* Sydney: Angus and Robertson, 1967. 305 pages.

Davis, Robert Gorham. *Ten Modern Masters: An Anthology of the Short Story,* third edition. New York: Harcourt Brace Jovanovich, 1972. 583 pages.

Day, Arthur Grove, ed. *The Art of Narration: The Short Story.* New York: McGraw-Hill, 1971. 438 pages.

—, ed. *The Greatest American Short Stories: Twenty Classics of Our Heritage.* New York: McGraw-Hill, 1953. 393 pages.

Dietrich, R. F., and Roger H. Sundell, eds. *The Art of Fiction: A Handbook and Anthology.* New York: Holt, Rinehart, and Winston, 1967. 445 pages.

Dolan, Paul J., eds. *Modes of Fiction.* New York: Free Press, 1970. 660 pages.

Dolley, Christopher, ed. *The Penguin Book of English Short Stories.* Harmondsworth: Penguin, 1967. 329 pages.

Durham, Philip, and Everett L. Jones, eds. *The Western Story: Fact, Fiction and Myth.* New York: Harcourt Brace Jovanovich, 1971. 369 pages.

Edwards, Don, ed. *At Home and Next Door: Australian and New Zealand Stories.* Sydney: Angus and Robertson, 1966. 103 pages.

Elkin, Stanley, ed. *Stories from the Sixties.* Garden City, New York: Doubleday, 1971. 400 pages.

Elliott, George P. *Types of Prose Fiction.* New York: Random House, 1964. 527 pages.

Eoff, Sherman, and Paul C. King, eds. *Spanish American Short Stories.* New York: Macmillan, 1963. 204 pages.

Esquire Editors. *The Best of Forty Years.* New York: David McKay, 1974. 352 pages.

Evans, Oliver, and Harry Finestone, eds. *The World of the Short Story: Archetypes in Action.* New York: A. A. Knopf, 1971. 581 pages.

Ewers, John Keith, ed. *Modern Australian Short Stories.* Melbourne: Georgian House, 1965. 202 pages.

Faderman, Lillian, and Barbara Bradshaw, eds. *Speaking for Ourselves: American Ethnic Writing.* Glenview, Illinois: Scott, Foresman, 1969. 615 pages.

Farris, Lester Collins, eds. *The Short Story: Studies in Creative Reading.* Kingsport Press, 1940. 390 pages.

Fenson, Harry, and Hildreth Kritzer, eds. *Reading, Understanding, and Writing about Stories.* New York: Free Press, 1966. 389 pages.

Ferguson, John De Lancey, *et al,* eds. *Theme and Variation in the Short Story.*

Figes, Eva, ed. *Modern Choice.* London: Blackie, 1966. 208 pages.

Finestone, Harry, and Oliver Evans, eds. *The World of the Short Story: Archetypes in Action.* New York: A. A. Knopf, 1971. 581 pages.

Firchow, Evelyn S., ed. and tr. *Icelandic Short Stories.* American Scandinavian Press, 1974.

Fitz Gerald, Gregory, ed. *Modern Satiric Stories: The Impropriety Principle.* Glenview, Illinois: Scott, Foresman, 1971. 472 pages.

Flores, Angel, ed. *Great Spanish Short Stories.* New York: Dell, 1962. 304 pages.

—, ed. *Nineteenth-Century French Tales.* New York: Ungar, 1967, c1960. 421 pages.

—, ed. *Nineteenth-Century German Tales.* New York: Ungar, 1966, c1959. 390 pages.

Flower, Dean, ed. *Counterparts: Classic and Contemporary American Short Stories.* Greenwich, Connecticut: Fawcett, 1971. 375 pages.

Foff, Arthur, and Daniel B. Knapp, eds. *Story: An Introduction to Prose Fiction,* 2nd ed. Belmont, California: Wadsworth Publishing Company, 1971. 521 pages.

Foley, Martha, and David Burnett, eds. *The Best American Short Stories: 1964-1971.* New York: Ballantine, 1964-1971.

Foley, Martha, ed. *The Best American Short Stories, 1972.*

Boston: Houghton Mifflin, 1972.

Foley, Martha, ed. *The Best American Short Stories, 1973.* New York: Random House, 1974.

—, ed. *The Best American Short Stories, 1974.* Boston: Houghton Mifflin, 1974.

Foley, Martha, and David Burnett, eds. *Best of the Best.* Boston: Houghton Mifflin, 1952.

—, eds. *Fifty Best American Short Stories: 1915-1965.* Boston: Houghton Mifflin, 1965.

Foley, Martha, ed. *Regional Stories from the Forty-Eight States.* New York: Random House, 1949.

Fowlie, Wallace, ed. *French Stories: A Bantam Dual-Language Book.* New York: Bantam, 1960. 333 pages.

Frakes, James R., and Isadore Traschen, eds. *Short Fiction: A Critical Collection,* 2nd ed. Englewood Cliffs, New Jersey: Prentice-Hall, 1969. 447 pages.

Franco, Jean, ed. *Short Stories in Spanish.* Harmondsworth, England: Penguin, 1966. 204 pages.

Frank, Joseph, ed. *You.* New York: Harcourt Brace Jovanovich, 1972. 281 pages.

Freidberg, Maurice, ed. *Russian Short Stories: A Bilingual Collection.* New York: Random House, 1964. 2 vols.

Garcia, Reloy, and Lloyd Hubenka, eds. *The Narrative Sensibility: An Introduction to Fiction.* New York: David McKay, 1975.

Gardner, John, and Dennis Dunlap, eds. *The Forms of Fiction.* New York: Random House, 1962. 657 pages.

Garrity, Devin A., ed. *Forty-Four Irish Short Stories.* New York: Devin-Adair, 1960, c1955. 500 pages.

Garrity, Devin A., ed. *Irish Stories and Tales.* New York: Pocket Books, 1956, c1955. 340 pages.

Gasarch, Ralph and Pearl, eds. *Fiction: The Universal Elements.* New York: Van Nostrand Reinhold, 1972. 456 pages.

Geist, Stanley, ed. *French Stories and Tales.* New York: Washington Square Press, 1967, c1954. 353 pages.

Gerber, Helmut E., ed. *The English Short Story in Transition: 1880-1920.* New York: Pegasus, 1967. 512 pages.

Gerstenberger, Donna, and Frederick Garber, eds. *Microcosm: An Anthology of the Short Story.* San Francisco: Chandler Publishing Company, 1969. 418 pages.

Gibian, George, and M. Samilov, eds. *Modern Russian Short Stories.* New York: Harper and Row, 1965. 380 pages.

Gilkes, Lillian, and Warren Bower, eds. *Short Story Craft.* New York: Macmillan, 1949. 501 pages.

Glazier, Teresa Ferster, ed. *Short Stories for Insight.* New York: Harcourt, Brace, 1967. 336 pages.

Gleeson, Patrick, ed. *A First Reader of American Short Fiction.* Columbus, Ohio: Merrill, 1971. 160 pages.

Glorfeld, Louis E., Robert N. Broadus, and Tom E. Kakonis, eds. *The Short Story: Ideas and Backgrounds.* Columbus, Ohio: Merrill, 1967. 316 pages.

Gohdes, Clarence, ed. *American Short Stories Series: 1832-1936.* 87 vols. Mss Information, 1974.

Gold, Herbert, ed. *Fiction of the Fifties.* Garden City, New York: Doubleday, 1959. 383 pages.

—, and David L. Stevenson, eds. *Stories of Modern America.* New York: St. Martin's Press, 1961. 441 pages.

Gold, Robert S., ed. *Point of Departure: Nineteen Stories of*

Youth and Discovery. New York: Dell, 1969, c1967. 190 pages.

Goldberg, Gerald, ed. *The Fate of Innocence.* Englewood Cliffs, New Jersey: Prentice-Hall, 1965. 271 pages.

Goldberg, Isaac, ed. and tr. *Brazilian Tales.* Boston: International Pocket Library, 1965, c1921. 96 pages.

Goldstone, Herbert I., Irving Cummings, and Thomas Churchill, eds. *Points of Departure: A Collection of Short Fiction.* Englewood Cliffs, New Jersey: Prentice-Hall, 1971. 512 pages.

Goldstone, Herbert I., ed. *The World's Best Short Short Stories.* New York: Bantam, 1967. 136 pages.

—, ed. *World-Wide Short Stories.* New York: Glober Book Company, 1966. 354 pages.

Gordon, Caroline, and Allen Tate, eds. *The House of Fiction,* 2nd ed. New York: Scribner's, 1960. 469 pages.

Gorodetzky, Nadejda, and Jessie Coulson, eds. *Russian Short Stories: Twentieth Century.* Oxford: Clarendon Press, 1965. 232 pages.

Graham, Stephen, ed. *Great Russian Short Stories.* New York: W. W. Norton, 1975. 1024 pages.

Graves, Wallace, and William G. Leary, eds. *From Word to Story.* New York: Harcourt Brace Jovanovich. 366 pages.

Green, Frederick Charles, ed. *French Short Stories of the Nineteenth and Twentieth Centuries.* New York: E. P. Dutton, 1933. 351 pages.

Greet, T. Y., Charles Edge, and John M. Munro, eds. *The Worlds of Fiction: Stories in Context.* Boston: Houghton Mifflin, 1964. 429 pages.

Gross, Beverly, and Richard Giannone, eds. *The Shapes of Fiction: Open and Closed.* New York: Holt, Rinehart, and

Winston, 1971. 434 pages.

Gross, Theodore, and Norman Kelvin, eds. *An Introduction to Literature: Fiction.* New York: Random House, 1967. 332 pages.

Grossman, William Leonard, ed. *Modern Brazilian Short Stories.* Berkeley: University of California Press, 1967. 167 pages.

Guerard, Albert Joseph, ed. *Stories of the Double.* Philadelphia: Lippincott, 1967. 331 pages.

Gullason, Thomas A., and Leonard Casper, eds. *The World of Short Fiction.* New York: Harper and Row, 1962. 546 pages.

Hadgraft, Cecil, and Richard Wilson, eds. *A Century of Australian Short Stories.* London: Heinemann, 1963. 336 pages.

Hale, Nancy, ed. *The Realities of Fiction.* London: Macmillan, 1963. 247 pages.

Hall, James B., ed. *The Realm of Fiction,* 2nd ed. New York: McGraw-Hill, 1970. 554 pages.

Hamalian, Leo, and Edmond L. Volpe, eds. *Nobel Prize Reader.* New York: Popular Library, 1965. 576 pages.

Hamalian, Leo, and Frederick R. Karl, eds. *The Shape of Fiction: British and American Short Stories.* New York: Mc-Graw-Hill, 1967. 448 pages.

—, eds. *Short Fiction of the Masters.* New York: Putnam, 1963. 447 pages.

Hardy, John Edward, ed. *The Modern Talent.* New York: Holt, Rinehart, and Winston, 1964. 502 pages.

Harper's Bazaar. The Uncommon Reader, ed. Alice S. Morris. New York: Avon, 1965. 416 pages.

Harrison, Constance, ed. *Short Stories.* Freeport, New York: Books for Libraries Press, 1969 reprint of 1893 edition. 220 pages.

Hartman, Carl, and Hazard Adams, eds. *Fiction as Process.* New York: Dodd, Mead, 1968. 371 pages.

Havighurst, ed. *Masters of the Modern Short Story.* New York: Harcourt, Brace, 1955. 453 pages.

Hayden, Robert, David J. Barrows, and Frederick Lapides, eds. *Afro-American Literature: An Introduction.* New York: Harcourt Brace Jovanovich, 1971. 309 pages.

Haydn, Hiram, and John Cournos, eds. *A World of Great Stories.* New York: Crown Publishers, 1947. 950 pages.

Heilman, Robert B., ed. *Modern Short Stories: A Critical Anthology.* Westport, Connecticut: Greenwood Press, 1971, c1950. 438 pages.

Heines, Donald S., ed. *Times Four: The Short Story in Depth.* Englewood Cliffs, New Jersey: Prentice-Hall, 1968. 379 pages.

Hemingway, Ernest, ed. *Men at War.* New York: Crown Publishers, 1942. 1072 pages.

Hemley, Elaine Gottlieb, and Jack Matthews, eds. *The Writer's Signature: Ideas in Story and Essay.* Glenview, Illinois: Scott, Foresman, 1972. 222 pages.

Hills, Penney Chapin, and L. Rust Hills, eds. *How We Live: Contemporary Life in Contemporary Fiction.* New York: Macmillan, 1968. 1008 pages.

Hills, L. Rust, ed. *Writer's Choice.* New York: David McKay Company, Inc., 1974. 456 pages.

Himber, David K., ed. *Toward Theme in Short Fiction.* Boston: Holbrook Press, 1973. 387 pages.

Hollander, John, ed. *American Short Stories Since 1945.* New

York: Harper and Row, 1968. 525 pages.

Hollander, Robert, and Sidney E. Lind, eds. *The Art of the Story.* New York: American Book Company, 1968. 405 pages.

Holm, Sven, ed. *Devil's Instrument and Other Danish Stories,* tr. Paula Hosrup-Jensen. Chester Springs, Pennsylvania: Dufour Editions, 1971. 266 pages.

Holmes, William, and Edward Mitchell, eds. *Nineteenth-Century American Short Fiction.* Glenview, Illinois: Scott, Foresman, 1970. 449 pages.

Holsinger, Rosemary, Camille Jordan, and Leon Levenson, eds. *The Creative Encounter.* Glenview, Illinois: Scott, Foresman, 1971. 373 pages.

Hondius, Katherine, ed. *Identity: Stories for This Generation.* Glenview, Illinois: Scott, Foresman, 1966. 288 pages.

Hopper, Vincent, ed. *Classic American Short Stories.* Great Neck, New York: Barron's Educational Series, 1964. 248 pages.

Houghton, Norris, ed. *Great Russian Short Stories.* New York: Dell, 1958. 383 pages.

Howard, C. Jeriel, and Richard F. Tracz, eds. *The Age of Anxiety: Modern American Stories.* Boston: Allyn and Bacon, 1972. 339 pages.

Howard, Daniel F., ed. *The Modern Tradition: An Anthology of Short Stories.* Boston: Little, Brown, 1968. 539 pages.

Howe, Irving, and Eliezer Greenburg, eds. *A Treasury of Yiddish Stories.* Greenwich, Connecticut: Fawcett, 1968, c1954. 512 pages.

—, eds. *Yiddish Stories, Old and New.* New York: Holiday House, 1974. 128 pages.

Howes, Barbara, and Gregory J. Smith, eds. *Sea-Green Horse: A Collection of Short Stories.* New York: Macmillan, 1970. 274 pages.

Howes, Barbara, ed. *Twenty-Three Modern Stories.* New York: Vintage Books, 1963. 395 pages.

Huberman, Edward and Elizabeth, eds. *Great British Short Stories.* New York: Bantam, 1968. 466 pages.

Huck, Wilbur, and William Shanhan, eds. *The Modern Short Story.* New York: American Book Company, 1968. 504 pages.

Hughes, Langston, ed. *The Best Short Stories by Negro Writers.* Boston: Little, Brown, 1967. 508 pages.

Hunter, Jim, ed. *Modern Short Stories.* London: Faber and Faber, 1966, c1964. 219 pages.

Hurtik, Emil, and Robert Yarber, eds. *An Introduction to Short Fiction and Criticism.* Waltham, Massachusetts: Xerox College Publications, 1971. 416 pages.

Iremonger, Valentin, ed. *Irish Short Stories.* London: Faber and Faber, 1960. 288 pages.

Isherwood, Christopher, ed. *Great English Short Stories.* New York: Dell, 1957. 416 pages.

Jaffe, Adrian H., and Virgil Scott, eds. *Studies in the Short Story,* 3rd ed. New York: Holt, Rinehart, Winston, 1968. 634 pages.

James, Brian, ed. *Australian Short Stories,* Second Series. London: Oxford University Press, 1963. 362 pages.

James, Charles L., ed. *From the Roots: Short Stories by Black Americans.* New York: Dodd, Mead, 1970. 370 pages.

Johnson, Ben, ed. *Stories of Modern Italy.* New York: Modern Library, 1960. 513 pages.

Johnson, Edward Warren, ed. *Short Stories International.* Boston: Houghton Mifflin, 1969. 406 pages.

Johnson, Eric W., ed. *Stories in Perspective.* Rochelle Park, New Jersey: Hayden, 1972. 256 pages.

Johnson, Willoughby, and William C. Hamlin, eds. *The Short Story.* New York: American Book Company, 1966. 342 pages.

Jolas, Eugene, and Robert Sage, eds. *Transition Stories: Twenty-Three Stories from Transition.* Freeport, New York: Books for Libraries Press, 1972 reprint of 1929 edition. 354 pages.

Jones, Phyllis M., ed. *Modern English Short Stories.* St. Clair Shores, Michigan: Scholarly Press, 1971 reprint of 1939 edition. 403 pages.

Kamen, Isai, ed. *Great Russian Stories.* New York: Random House, 1959. 311 pages.

Kane, Thomas S., and Leonard J. Peterson, eds. *The Short Story and the Reader.* London and New York: Oxford University Press, 1976. 544 pages.

Karl, Frederick R., and Leo Hamalian, eds. *The Naked I: Fictions for the Seventies.* Greenwich, Connecticut: Fawcett, 1971. 374 pages.

Kelley, Leo P., ed. *Fantasy: The Literature of the Marvelous.* New York: McGraw-Hill, 1974. 312 pages.

Kempton, Kenneth P., ed. *Short Stories for Study.* Cambridge, Massachusetts: Harvard University Press, 1953. 351 pages.

—, ed. *The Supernatural in Fiction.* New York: McGraw-Hill, 1973. 324 pages.

—., ed. *Themes in Science Fiction.* New York: McGraw-Hill, 1972. 428 pages.

Kennedy, James G., ed. *Stories East and West.* Glenview, Illinois: Scott, Foresman, 1971. 311 pages.

Kenner, Hugh. *Studies in Change: A Book of the Short Story.* Englewood Cliffs, New Jersey: Prentice-Hall, 1965. 328 pages.

Kermode, Frank, ed. *The Sense of an Ending: Studies in the Theory of Fiction.* London and New York: Oxford University Press, 1974.

Kernan, Alvin B., Peter B. Brooks, and J. Michael Holquist, eds. *Man and His Fictions: An Introduction to Fiction Making, Its Forms and Uses.* New York: Harcourt Brace Jovanovich, 1973. 534 pages.

Kielty, Bernardine, ed. *A Treasury of Short Stories.* New York: Simon and Schuster, 1947. 849 pages.

Kimball, Rodney A., ed. *The Short Story Reader.* New York: Odyssey Press, 1961. 460 pages.

Kimmey, John L., ed. *Experience and Expression: Reading and Responding to Short Fiction.* Glenview, Illinois: Scott, Foresman, 1976. 516 pages.

—, ed. *An Introduction to Short Fiction.* Glenview, Illinois: Scott, Foresman, 1976. 512 pages.

King, Woodie, ed. *Black Short Story Anthology.* New York: Columbia University Press, 1972. 381 pages.

Klein, Marcus, and Robert Pack, eds. *Short Stories: Classic, Modern, Contemporary.* Boston: Little, Brown, 1967. 606 pages.

Klinkowitz, Jerome, and John Somer, eds. *Innovative Fiction: Stories for the Seventies.* New York: Dell, 1975. n.p.

Klotz, Marvin, and Richard Abcarian, eds. *The Experience of Fiction.* New York: St. Martin's Press, 1975.

Konigsberg, Ira, ed. *The Classic Short Story.* New York: Harper and Row, 1971. 446 pages.

Kostelanetz, Richard, ed. *Twelve from the Sixities.* New York: Dell, 1967. 272 pages.

Kytle, Ray, and Annette Peterson Kytle, eds. *The Complex Vision: A Collection of Short Stories.* New York: Harcourt Brace Jovanovich, 1972. 307 pages.

Lambert, Robert, ed. *The Tunnel and the Light: Readings in Modern Fiction.* Boston: Houghton Mifflin, 1971. 352 pages.

Lange, Victor, ed. *Great German Short Novels and Stories.* New York: Modern Library, 1952. 486 pages.

Langland, Joseph, and James P. Hall, eds. *The Short Story.* New York: Macmillan, 1956. 485 pages.

Larsen, Hanna A., ed. *Norway's Best Stories: An Introduction to Modern Norwegian Fiction,* tr. Anders Orbeck. Freeport, New York: Books for Libraries Press, 1971 reprint of 1927 edition. 369 pages.

—, ed. *Sweden's Best Short Stories: An Introduction to Swedish Fiction,* tr. Charles Wharton Stork. Freeport, New York: Books for Libraries Press, 1971 reprint of 1927 edition. 365 pages.

Lass, Abraham, and Norma Tasman, eds. *"The Secret Sharer" and Other Great Stories.* New York: New American Library, 1969. 352 pages.

—, eds. *Twenty-One Great Stories.* New York: New American Library, 1969. 352 pages.

Lawaetz, Gudie, ed. *Spanish Short Stories.* Harmondsworth, England: Penguin, 1972. 2 vols.

Lee, Simon, ed. *French Short Stories.* Harmondsworth, England: Penguin, 1972. 2 vols.

Leecing, Walden, and James L. Armstrong, eds. *The Curious Eye.* New York: McGraw-Hill, 1970. 528 pages.

Lesser, M. X., and John N. Morris, eds. *Modern Short Stories: The Fiction of Experience.* New York: McGraw-Hill, 1962. 460 pages.

Levin, Gerald, ed. *The Short Story: An Inductive Approach.* New York: Harcourt, Brace, and World, 1967. 520 pages.

Lid, Richard Wald, ed. *The Short Story: Classic and Contemporary.* Philadelphia: Lippincott, 1966. 538 pages.

Lieberman, Elias, ed. *The American Short Story.* Ridgewood, New Jersey: The Editor, 1912. 183 pages.

Lighthall, Nancy, ed. *Point of View.* Follet, 1973. 3 vols.

Linscott, Robert N., ed. *The Best American Humorous Short Stories.* New York: Random House, 1945. 436 pages.

Lish, Gordon, ed. *The Secret Life of Our Times: New Fiction from Esquire.* New York: Doubleday, 1973. 641 pages.

Lucas, Alec, ed. *Great Canadian Short Stories: An Anthology.* New York: Dell, 1971.

Ludwig, Jack, and W. Richard Poirier, eds. *Stories: British and American.* Boston: Houghton Mifflin, 1953. 505 pages.

Lynskey, Winifred, ed. *Reading Modern Fiction: 31 Stories with Critical Aids*, 4th ed. New York: Scribner's, 1968. 541 pages.

Lyon, Pamela, ed. *French Short Stories.* Baltimore: Penguin, 1966. 276 pages.

Mabie, Hamilton Wright, ed. *Short Stories in Literature.* New York: Dodd, Mead and Company, 1891. 201 pages.

McClennen, Joshua, ed. *Masters and Masterpieces of the Short Story*, First Series. New York: Holt, Rinehart and Winston, 1957. 235 pages.

—, ed. *Masters and Masterpieces of the Short Story*, Second Series. New York: Holt, Rinehart and Winston, 1960. 562

pages.

McEvoy, Bernard L., ed. *Stories from Across Canada.* Philadelphia: Lippincott, 1967, c1966. 100 pages.

McHargue, Georgess, ed. *The Best of Both Worlds: An Anthology of Stories for All Ages.* Garden City, New York: Doubleday, 1968. 773 pages.

McKenzie, Barbara, ed. *The Process of Fiction,* 2nd ed. New York: Harcourt, Brace, 1974. 611 pages.

Magalaner, Marvin, and Edmond Volpe, eds. *Twelve Short Stories,* First Series. New York: Macmillan, 1961. 314 pages.

—, eds. *Twelve Short Stories,* Second Series. New York: Macmillan, 1969. 290 pages.

Male, Roy R., ed. *Types of Short Fiction.* Belmont, California: Wadsworth, 1970. 563 pages.

Malin, Irving, ed. *Psychoanalysis and American Fiction.* New York: E. P. Dutton, 1965. 316 pages.

Mansfield, Roger, ed. *Subjects of Inquiry: A Book of Modern Short Stories.* London: Blackie, 1967. 134 pages.

Marcus, Fred H., ed. *Perception and Pleasure: Stories for Analysis.* Boston: D. C. Heath, 1968, c1967. 281 pages.

Marcus, Steven, ed. *The World of Modern Fiction.* New York: Simon and Schuster, 1966. 2 vols.

Marielle, Edward, ed. *The Penguin Book of French Short Stories.* Harmondsworth, England: Penguin, 1968. 408 pages.

Mason, William Heppell, ed. *Stories and Afterthoughts.* Oxford: Blackwell, 1966. 152 pages.

Marx, Paul, ed. *Twelve Short Story Writers.* New York: Holt, Rinehart, and Winston, 1970. 451 pages.

Matlaw, Myron, and Leonard Lief, eds. *Story and Critic.* New York: Harper and Row, 1963. 357 pages.

Maugham, Somerset, ed. *Tellers of Tales.* Garden City, New York: Doubleday, 1939. 1526 pages.

Mellard, James M., ed. *Four Models: A Rhetoric of Modern Fiction.* New York: Macmillan, 1973. 526 pages.

Mercier, Vivian, ed. *Great Irish Short Stories.* New York: Dell, 1964. 384 pages.

Meredith, Michael, ed. *Twentieth-Century Story and Statement.* London; Toronto: Harrap, 1967. 152 pages.

Mikels, Rosa M., and Helen T. Munn, eds. *Short Stories for English Courses.* New York: Scribner's, 1960. 553 pages.

Miller, James E., Jr., and Bernice Slote, eds. *The Dimensions of the Short Story.* New York: Dodd, Mead, 1964. 564 pages.

Miller, James E., Jr., ed. *Myth and Method: Modern Theories of Fiction.* Lincoln: University of Nebraska Press, 1960. 165 pages.

Millett, Fred B., ed. *Reading Fiction: A Method of Analysis with Selections for Study.* New York: Harper, 1950. 269 pages.

Mills, Nicolaus, ed. *Comparisons: A Short Story Anthology.* New York: McGraw-Hill, 1972. 416 pages.

Minot, Stephen, and Robley Wilson, Jr., eds. *Three Stances of Modern Fiction: A Critical Anthology of the Short Story.* Englewood Cliffs, New Jersey: Prentice-Hall, 1972. 307 pages.

Mirer, Martin, ed. *Modern Black Stories.* Woodbury, New York: Barron's Educational Series, 1971. 196 pages.

Mitchell, Edward, and Rainer Schulte, eds. *Continental Short Stories: The Modern Tradition.* New York: W. W. Norton,

1968. 176 pages.

Mitford, Mary Russell, ed. *Stories of American Life, by American Writers.* New York: Garrett Press, 1969 reprint of nineteenth-century edition. 3 vols.

Mizener, Arthur, ed. *Modern Short Stories: The Uses of Imagination,* third edition. New York: W. W. Norton, 1971. 824 pages.

Moffett, James, and Kenneth R. McElheny, eds. *Points of View: An Anthology of Short Stories.* New York: New American Library, 1966. 576 pages.

Momaday, Natachee, ed. *American Indian Authors.* Boston: Houghton Mifflin, 1972. 151 pages.

Moody, Harold Leonard Birch, ed. *Facing Facts: A Book of Twentieth-Century Stories.* London: Blackie, 1966. 137 pages.

Morris, John Ifor, ed. *Short Stories Since 1930: A Selection from the British Isles.* London: R. Hart-Davis, 1965. 123 pages.

Morris, Rosamund, ed. *Great Detective Stories.* New York: Hart, 1965. 191 pages.

—, ed. *Great Horror Stories.* New York: Hart, 1965. 191 pages.

—, ed. *Masterpieces of Humor.* New York: Hart, 1966. 256 pages.

—, ed. *Masterpieces of Mystery and Deduction.* New York: Hart, 1966, c1965. 256 pages.

—, ed. *Masterpieces of Suspense.* New York: Hart, 1966. 254 pages.

Morse, Donald. *The Choices of Fiction.* Englewood Cliffs, New Jersey: Prentice-Hall, 1974. 384 pages.

Morton, Miriam, tr. *Voices from France: Ten Stories by French Nobel Prize Winners.* Garden City, New York: Doubleday, 1969. 212 pages.

Murphy, Geraldine, ed. *Momentary Stay: A Short Story Collection.* New York: Harper and Row, 1972. 462 pages.

Nagel, James, ed. *Vision and Value: A Thematic Introduction to the Short Story.* Belmont, California: Dickenson Publishing Company, 1970. 382 pages.

Nathan, Norman, ed. *Short Stories: An Anthology.* Indianapolis: Bobs-Merrill, 1969. 341 pages.

Neider, Charles, ed. *Great Short Stories from the World's Literature,* enlarged edition. New York: Holt, Rinehart and Winston, 1972. 553 pages.

Nemcová, Jeanne W., ed. and tr. *Czech and Slovak Short Stories.* New York and London: Oxford University Press, 1967. 296 pages.

Nettleton, George H., ed. *Specimens of the Short Story.* Freeport, New York: Books for Libraries Press, 1969 reprint of 1901 edition. 229 pages.

The New Yorker. Stories from The New Yorker. New York: Simon and Schuster, 1965. 3 vols.

Newnham, Richard, ed. *German Short Stories.* Baltimore: Penguin, 1964. 175 pages.

—, ed. *Soviet Short Stories.* Baltimore: Penguin, 1963. 223 pages.

Oates, Joyce Carol, ed. *Scenes from American Life: Contemporary Short Fiction.* New York: Vanguard Press, 1973. 271 pages.

O'Brien, Edward J., ed. *The Best British Short Stories of 1922-1927.* New York: Dodd, Mead, 1928. 6 vols.

—, ed. *The Best British Short Stories of 1933-1940.* Boston:

Houghton Mifflin, 1940. 8 vols.

O'Brien, Edward J., ed. *Elizabethan Tales.* Boston: Houghton Mifflin, 1937. 317 pages.

—, ed. *Fifty Best American Short Stories 1915-1939.* Boston: Houghton Mifflin, 1939. 868 pages.

—, ed. *The Short Story Case Book.* New York: Farrar, 1935. 635 pages.

—, ed. *Twenty-Five Finest Short Stories.* New York: Farrar, 1931. 513 pages.

O'Connor, Frank, ed. *The Lonely Voice: A Study of the Short Story.* New York: Bantam, 1968, c1963. 220 pages.

O'Faolain, Sean, ed. *Short Stories: A Study in Pleasure.* Boston: Little, Brown, 1961. 496 pages.

Olmsted, Richard H., and Raymond L. Grismer, eds. *Spanish Short Stories.* New York: Ronald Press, 1942. 306 pages.

De Onís, Harriet, ed. *Spanish Stories and Tales.* New York: Washington Square, 1962, c1956. 288 pages.

Orlovitz, Gil, ed. *The Award Avant-Garde Reader.* New York: Award Books, 1965. 254 pages.

Pacey, Desmond, ed. *A Book of Canadian Stories.* Toronto: Ryerson Press, 1967. 346 pages.

Pargment, Lila, ed. and tr. *The Girl from Moscow, and Other Stories.* New York: Ungar, 1968. 170 pages.

Parker, Dorothy, and Frederick B. Shroyer, eds. *Short Story: A Thematic Anthology.* New York: Scribner's, 1965. 462 pages.

Pasinetti, P. M., ed. *Great Italian Short Stories.* New York: Dell, 1959. 412 pages.

Peden, William Harwood, ed. *The American Short Story.* Boston: Houghton Mifflin, 1964. 213 pages.

—, ed. *The Golden Shore: Great Short Stories Selected for Young Readers.* New York: Platt and Munk, 1967. 339 pages.

—, ed. *Short Fiction: Shape and Substance.* Boston: Houghton Mifflin, 1971. 556 pages.

—, ed. *Twenty-Nine Stories.* Boston: Houghton Mifflin, 1967. 374 pages.

Penzoldt, P., ed. *The Supernatural in Fiction.* New York: Humanities Press, 1965, c1952. 271 pages.

Perkins, George, ed. *Realistic American Short Fiction.* Glenview, Illinois: Scott-Foresman, 1972. 416 pages.

Perrine, Laurence, ed. *Story and Structure,* fourth edition. New York: Harcourt Brace Jovanovich, 1974. 560 pages.

Pick, Robert, ed. *German Stories and Tales.* New York: Washington Square, 1962, c1954. 399 pages.

Pickering, James H., ed. *Fiction 100: An Anthology of Short Stories.* New York: Macmillan, 1974. 1048 pages.

Pomorska, Krystyna, ed. *Fifty Years of Russian Prose: From Pasternak to Solzhenitsyn.* Cambridge: Massachusetts Institute of Technology, 1971. 2 vols.

Prescott, Orville, ed. *Mid-Century: An Anthology of Distinguished Contemporary American Short Stories.* New York: Washington Square Press, 1971, c1958. 320 pages.

Proffer, Carl R., ed. *From Karamzin to Bunin: An Anthology of Russian Short Stories.* Bloomington: Indiana University Press, 1969. 468 pages.

Purcell, Mary, and Robert C. Wylder, eds. *The Narrative Impulse: Short Stories for Analysis.* New York: Odyssey Press, 1963. 255 pages.

Rabikovitz, Dalia, ed. *The New Israeli Writers: Short Stories of the First Generation.* New York: Funk and Wagnalls, 1969. 319 pages.

Ravitz, Abe C., ed. *The American Disinherited: A Profile in Fiction.* Belmont, California: Dickenson Publishing Company, 1970. 238 pages.

Reavey, George, ed. *Fourteen Great Short Stories by Soviet Authors.* New York: Avon, 1959. 224 pages.

Rees, Robert A., and Barry Menikoff, eds. *The Short Story: An Introductory Anthology.* Boston: Little, Brown, 1969. 632 pages.

Reeve, F. D., ed. *Great Soviet Short Stories.* New York: Dell, 1962. 480 pages.

Rehder, Jessie. *The Story at Work: An Anthology.* New York: Odyssey Press, 1963. 404 pages.

Reid, James Macarthur, ed. *Scottish Short Stories.* London and Oxford: Oxford University Press, 1963. 328 pages.

Rideout, Albert K., and Jesse Stuart, eds. *Short Stories for Discussion.* New York: Scribner's, 1965. 489 pages.

Rimanelli, Giose, and Roberto Ruberto, eds. *Modern Canadian Stories.* Toronto: Ryerson Press, 1966. 402 pages.

Roecker, William A., ed. *Stories That Count.* New York: Holt, Rinehart and Winston, 1971. 214 pages.

Rosenfeld, Max, ed. and tr. *Pushcarts and Dreamers: Stories of Jewish Life in America.* South Brunswick, New Jersey: T. Yoseloff, 1969, c1967. 221 pages.

—, ed. *A Union for Shabbos and Other Stories of Jewish Life in America.* Philadelphia: Sholom Aleichem Club Press, 1967. 221 pages.

Ross, Woodburn O., and A. Dayle Wallace, eds. *Short Stories in

Context.   New York: American Book Company, 1953. 368 pages.

Sachs, Murray, ed. *The French Short Story in the Nineteenth Century.* New York: Oxford University Press, 1969. 403 pages.

Sanders, Thomas E., ed. *The Discovery of Fiction.* Glenview, Illinois: Scott, Foresman, 1967. 699 pages.

Satin, Joseph, ed. *Reading Prose Fiction.* New York: Houghton Mifflin, 1964. 329 pages.

The Saturday Evening Post. Best Modern Short Stories, Selected from the Saturday Evening Post. New York: Curtis Books, 1965. 494 pages.

—. *The Saturday Evening Post Stories, 1942-1945,* ed. Ben Hibbs. New York: Random House, 1946. 4 vols.

—. *The Saturday Evening Post Stories, 1946-1952,* published in New York, by Random House, in 1947, 1948, 1949, 1950, 1951, 1952, one volume per year. 6 vols.

Saul, George Brandon, ed. *Owls' Watch.* Greenwich, Connecticut: Fawcett, 1965. 238 pages.

Scheld, Elizabeth, ed. *Designs in Fiction.* New York: Macmillan, 1968. 256 pages.

Schneiderman, Beth Kline, ed. *By and About Women: An Anthology of Short Fiction.* New York: Harcourt Brace Jovanovich, 1973. 337 pages.

Schorer, Mark, ed. *The Story: A Critical Anthology,* 2nd ed. Englewood Cliffs, New Jersey: Prentice-Hall, 1967. 459 pages.

Schulman, L. M., ed. *The Loners: Short Stories about the Young Alienated.* New York: Macmillan, 1970. 279 pages.

—, ed. *Travelers: Stories of Americans Abroad.* New York: Macmillan, 1972. 286 pages.

Schulz, Max, ed. *Black Humor Fiction of the Sixties.* Athens, Ohio: Ohio University Press, 1975. 156 pages.

Schweitzer, John C., ed. *Discovering Short Stories.* New York: Scribner's, 1968. 184 pages.

—, ed. *Variety of Short Stories.* New York: Scribner's, 1968. 184 pages.

Scoggin, Margaret C., ed. *Chucklebait: Funny Stories for Everyone.* New York: Dell, 1964. 285 pages.

Scott, Virgil, ed. *Studies in the Short Story*, alternate edition. New York: Holt, Rinehart and Winston, 1971. 654 pages.

Scriabine, Helene, ed. *Short Stories by Pushkin, Lermontov, and Dostoyevsky.* New York: Harper, 1965. 137 pages.

Selected English Short Stories, Nineteenth Century, First Series. London and New York: Oxford University Press, 1974.

Selected English Short Stories, Nineteenth and Twentieth Centuries, Second Series. London and New York: Oxford University Press, 1974.

Seven Icelandic Short Stories. Reykjavik, Iceland: The Ministry of Education, 1960. 166 pages.

Shaw, Harry, and Douglas Bement, eds. *Reading the Short Story.* New York: Harper, 1954. 396 pages.

Sherman, Stuart P., ed. *A Book of Short Stories.* Freeport, New York: Books for Libraries Press, 1971 reprint of 1914 edition. 353 pages.

Short, Raymond W., and R. B. Sewall, eds. *Short Stories for Study.* New York: Holt, Rinehart and Winston, 1956. 618 pages.

Singer, Kurt D., ed. *Famous Short Stories.* Minneapolis: Dennison, 1968. n.p.

Singleton, Ralph H., ed. *The Art of Prose Fiction.* Cleveland: World, 1967. 109 pages.

—, ed. *Two and Twenty: A Collection of Short Stories.* New York: St. Martin's, 1962. 434 pages.

Sklare, Arnold, and William E. Buckler, eds. *Stories from Six Authors.* New York: McGraw-Hill, 1966. 417 pages.

Smart, William, ed. *Women and Men, Men and Women.* New York: St. Martin's, 1976. 405 pages.

Sohn, David A., ed. *Ten Modern American Short Stories.* New York: Bantam, 1965. 154 pages.

—, ed. *Ten Top Stories.* New York: Bantam, 1964. 168 pages.

Somer, John, ed. *Narrative Experience: The Private Voice.* Glenview, Illinois: Scott, Foresman, 1970. 188 pages.

Speare, Morris E., ed. *The Pocket Book of Short Stories.* New York: Pocket Books, 1957. 338 pages.

Spender, Stephen, ed. *Great German Short Stories.* New York: Dell, 1960. 284 pages.

Stanford, Derek, ed. *Short Stories of the 'Nineties.* New York: Roy, 1969, c1968. 252 pages.

Stansbury, D. L., ed. *Impact: Short Stories for Pleasure.* Englewood Cliffs, New Jersey: Prentice-Hall, 1971. 377 pages.

Stanton, Robert, ed. *The Short Story and the Reader.* New York: Holt, Rinehart and Winston, 1960. 557 pages.

Stegner, Wallace and Mary, eds. *Great American Short Stories.* New York: Dell, 1957. 511 pages.

Stegner, Wallace, ed. *The Writer's Art: A Collection of Short Stories.* Westport, Connecticut: Greenwood Press, 1972, c1950. 358 pages.

Stein, Allen F., and Thomas N. Walters, eds. *The Southern Ex-*

perience in Short Fiction. Glenview, Illinois: Scott, Foresman, 1971. 260 pages.

Steinhauer, Harry, ed. *German Stories: A Bantam Dual-Language Book.* New York: Bantam, 1974.

Stephens, Donald, ed. *Contemporary Voices: The Short Story in Canada.* Scarborough, Ontario: Prentice-Hall, of Canada, 1972. 186 pages.

Stern, Philip Van Doren, ed. *The Pocket Book of Modern American Short Stories.* New York: Washington Square Press, 1963. 293 pages.

Sterner, Lewis George, ed. *American Short Stories.* New York: Globe Book Company, 1966. 559 pages.

Stevick, Philip, ed. *Anti-Story: An Anthology of Experimental Fiction.* New York: Free Press, 1971. 319 pages.

Stone, Wilfred, and Nancy Huddleston Parker, eds. *The Short Story: An Introduction.* New York: McGraw-Hill, 1976. 608 pages.

Stories by Foreign Authors. Freeport, New York: Books for Libraries Press, 1970 reprint of 1898 edition. 7 vols.

Stories by Jean Stafford et al, ed. William Peden. New York: Farrar, Straus and Giroux, 1966. 309 pages.

Story. Story, the Fiction of the Forties, ed. Whit and Hallie Burnett. New York: Dutton, 1949. 620 pages.

The Story Today, 1966/1967: From England, Italy, Germany, France, United States, Finland, Holland, Denmark, and Sweden. New York: Simon and Schuster, 1967. 254 pages.

Strahan, John W. *Fifteen Great Russian Short Stories.* New York: Washington Square, 1965. 295 pages.

Suits, Conrad B., ed. *Stories for Writing.* New York: Harper and Row, 1971. 407 pages.

Swallow, Alan, ed. *Anchor in the Sea: An Anthology of Psychological Fiction.* Denver: Alan Swallow Press, 1966, c1947. 363 pages.

Taylor, John Chesley, ed. *The Short Story: Fiction in Transition.* New York: Scribner's, 1969. 638 pages.

Taylor, J. Golden, ed. *Great Short Stories of the West.* New York: Ballantine, 1974. 2 vols.

Thorburn, David, ed. *Initiation: Stories and Short Novels on Three Themes.* New York: Harcourt Brace Jovanovich, 1971. 368 pages.

Thube, Ensaf and Ruth Prigozy, eds. *Short Stories: A Critical Anthology.* New York: Macmillan, 1973. 615 pages.

Thurston, Jarvis A., ed. *Reading Modern Short Stories.* Glenview, Illinois: Scott, Foresman, 1955. 728 pages.

—, and Curt Johnson, eds. *Short Stories from the Literary Magazines.* Glenview, Illinois: Scott, Foresman, 1970. 444 pages.

Timko, Michael, and Clinton F. Oliver, eds. *38 Short Stories: An Introductory Anthology.* New York: Knopf, 1968. 735 pages.

Trevelyan, Raleigh, ed. *Italian Short Stories.* Baltimore: Penguin, 1965. 197 pages.

Turner, Arlin, ed. *Southern Stories.* New York: Holt, Rinehart and Winston, 1960. 336 pages.

Turner, Darwin T., ed. *Black American Literature: Fiction.* Columbus, Ohio: Merrill, 1969. 142 pages.

Turner, James, ed. *A Coin Has Two Sides: A Collection of Double Stories on the Theme of Love.* London: Cassell, 1967. 239 pages.

Tytell, John, and Harold Jaffe, eds. *Affinities: A Short Story Anthology.* New York: Crowell, 1970. 468 pages.

Underwood, Edna W., ed. *Famous Stories from Foreign Countries.* Boston: International Pocket Library, 1964, c1921. 111 pages.

—, ed. *Short Stories from the Balkans.* New York: AMS Press, 1970 reprint of 1919 edition. 246 pages.

Vittorini, Dimitri, ed. *Italian Short Stories.* Harmondsworth, England: Penguin, 1972. 208 pages.

Waidson, H. M., ed. *German Short Stories.* Cambridge: Cambridge University Press, 1974. 3 vols.

Waldhorn, Arthur, and Hilda, eds. *The Rite of Becoming: Stories and Studies of Adolescence.* Cleveland: World, 1966. 292 pages.

Waldman, Guido, ed. *The Penguin Book of Italian Short Stories.* Baltimore: Penguin, 1969. 335 pages.

Waldmeir, Joseph J., ed. *Recent American Fiction: Some Critical Views.* Boston: Houghton Mifflin, 1963. 292 pages.

Warfel, Harry R., and G. H. Orians, eds. *American Local-Color Stories.* New York: Cooper Square, 1970, c1941. 846 pages.

Warren, Robert Penn, and Albert Erskine, eds. *Short Story Masterpieces.* New York: Dell, 1966, c1954. 542 pages.

Warren, Robert Penn, ed. *A Southern Harvest.* Dunwoody, Georgia: N. S. Berg, 1972, c1937. 359 pages.

Wassner, Selig O., ed. and tr. *Treasury of Russian Short Stories, 1900-1966.* New York: F. Fell, 1968. 315 pages.

Waten, Judah, and Stephen Murray-Smith, eds. *Classic Australian Short Stories.* Melbourne: Wren Publishers, 1974. 352 pages.

Weaver, Robert, ed. *Canadian Short Stories.* Toronto: Oxford University Press, First Series, 1966 (420 pages); Second

Series, 1968 (378 pages).

Weimer, David R., ed. *Modern American Classics.* New York: Random House, 1969. 463 pages.

Weiss, Morton Jerome, ed. *Tales out of School.* New York: Dell, 1967. 158 pages.

Welker, Robert L., and Herschel Gower, eds. *The Sense of Fiction.* Englewood Cliffs, New Jersey: Prentice-Hall, 1966. 457 pages.

West, Ray B., Jr., and Robert W. Stallman, eds. *The Art of Modern Fiction.* New York: Holt, Rinehart and Winston, 1962, c1949. 652 pages.

West, Ray B., Jr., ed. *Reading the Short Story.* New York: Crowell, 1968. 239 pages.

—, ed. *The Short Story in America.* Freeport, New York: Books for Libraries Press, 1968, c1952. 147 pages.

West, Theodore, ed. *The Continental Short Story: An Existential Approach.* New York: Odyssey Press, 1969. 483 pages.

Whitehead, Frank S., ed. *Mainstream: Modern Short Stories.* London: Chatto and Windus, 1967. 2 vols.

Williams, Blanche Colton, ed. *O. Henry Memorial Award Prize Stories of 1925-1932.* Garden City, New York: Doubleday, 1925-1932. 8 vols.

Wilson, Richard, ed. *English Short Stories: Fifteenth to Twentieth Centuries.* New York: Dutton, 1974.

Woollcott, Alexander, ed. *The Woollcott Reader.* New York: Viking, 1935. 1010 pages.

Wright, Austin M., ed. *The American Short Story in the Twenties.* Chicago: University of Chicago Press, 1961. 425 pages.

Yarmolinsky, Avrahm, ed. *Treasury of Great Russian Short*

Stories: Pushkin to Gorky, 2nd ed. New York: Macmillan, 1947, c1944. 1018 pages.

IV. MIXED-GENRE ANTHOLOGIES
CONTAINING THE SHORT STORY:

Abcarian, Richard, and Marvin Klotz, eds. *Literature: The Human Experience.* New York: St. Martin's Press, 1973. 971 pages.

Austin, Lettie J., Lewis H. Fenderson, and Sophia P. Nelson, eds. *The Black Man and the Promise of America.* Glenview, Illinois: Scott, Foresman, 1970. 523 pages.

Bain, Carl E., Jerome Beaty, and J. Paul Hunter, eds. *The Norton Introduction to Literature,* combined shorter edition. New York: W. W. Norton and Company, Inc., 1973. 1191 pages.

Barnet, Sylvan, Morton Berman, and William Burto, eds. *An Introduction to Literature.* Boston: Little, Brown, 1974.

Beal, Richard S., and Jacob Korg, eds. *The Complete Reader.* Englewood Cliffs, New Jersey: Prentice-Hall, 1967. 627 pages.

Beardsley, Monroe C., Robert W. Daniel, and Glenn Leggett, eds. *Theme and Form: An Introduction to Literature,* 3rd ed. Englewood Cliffs, New Jersey: Prentice-Hall, 1969. 756 pages.

Bell, James K., and Adrian A. Cohn, eds. *Rhetoric in a Modern Mode, with Selected Readings.* Beverly Hills, California: Glencoe Press, 1972. 424 pages.

Berg, Stephen, S. J. Marks, and J. Michael Pilz, eds. *Between People: A Reader for Open Learning.* Glenview, Illinois: Scott, Foresman, 1972. 511 pages.

Bierman, Judah, James Hart, and Stanley Johnson, eds. *The Treehouse: An Introduction to Literature.* Cambridge, Massachusetts: Winthrop Publishers, 1974.

Blair, Walter, John Gerber, and Eugene K. Garber, eds. *Better Reading II: Literature,* fourth edition. Glenview, Illinois: Scott, Foresman, 1966. 830 pages.

Blair, Walter, and John Gerber, eds. *Repertory.* Glenview, Illinois: Scott, Foresman, 1968. 1191 pages.

Brooks, Cleanth, John Thibaut Purser, and Robert Penn Warren, eds. *Approaches to Literature,* fourth edition. New York: Appleton-Century-Crofts, 1964. 917 pages.

Cohen, B. Bernard, ed. *Literature for Understanding.* Glenview, Illinois: Scott, Foresman, 1966. 530 pages.

Connolly, Francis, ed. *Man and His Measure.* New York: Harcourt Brace Jovanovich, 1964. 1394 pages.

Corder, Jim W., ed. *Finding a Voice.* Glenview, Illinois: Scott, Foresman, 1973. 796 pages.

Cox, Martha Heasley, ed. *Image and Value: An Invitation to Literature.* New York: Harcourt Brace Jovanovich, 1966. 630 pages.

Craft, Harvey M., ed. *Logic, Style, and Arrangement: Literature for Composition.* Beverly Hills, California: Glencoe Press, 1971. 520 pages.

Davis, Muriel, ed. *Inscape: Stories, Plays and Poems.* Philadelphia: Lippincott, 1971. 632 pages.

De Nitto, Dennis, and Daniel J. Leary, eds. *Contrasts.* New York: Macmillan, 1969. 444 pages.

Dodge, Richard H., and Peter D. Lindblom, eds. *Of Time and Experience: Literary Themes.* Englewood Cliffs, New Jersey: Prentice-Hall (Winthrop), 1972. 725 pages.

Doherty, Joseph F., and William Stephenson, eds. *The Inward

Journey. New York: Harcourt Brace Jovanovich, 1973. 437 pages.

Doster, William C., ed. *The Differing Eye: An Introduction to Literature.* Beverly Hills, California: Glencoe Press, 1970. 320 pages.

Duhamel, P. Albert, and Richard E. Hughes, eds. *Literature: Form and Function.* Englewood Cliffs, New Jersey: Prentice-Hall, 1965. 635 pages.

Faderman, Lillian, and Barbara Bradshaw, eds. *Speaking for Ourselves.* Glenview, Illinois: Scott, Foresman, 1975. 625 pages.

Farrell, Edmund James, and others. *Exploring Life Through Literature.* Glenview, Illinois: Scott, Foresman, 1973. 626 pages.

Francis, Nelle, and J. Warren Smith, eds. *Patterns for Prose Writing: From Notes to Theme.* Glenview, Illinois: Scott, Foresman, 1969. 344 pages.

Gangewere, Robert J., ed. *The Exploited Eden: Literature on the American Environment.* New York: Harper and Row, 1972. 396 pages.

Gillespie, Sheena, and Linda Stanley, eds. *The Treehouse: An Introduction to Literature.* Englewood Cliffs, New Jersey: Prentice-Hall, 1974. 384 pages.

—, eds. *Someone Like Me: A Rhetorical Reader.* Englewood Cliffs, New Jersey: Prentice-Hall, 1973. 352 pages.

Gordon, Walter K., ed. *Literature in Critical Perspectives: An Anthology.* New York: Appleton-Century-Crofts, 1968. 795 pages.

Graham, Cary B., ed. *Freshman English Program.* Chicago: Scott, Foresman, 1960. 946 pages.

Guerin, Wilfred L. *et al,* eds. *Mandala: Literature for Critical Analysis.* New York: Harper and Row, 1970. 766 pages.

Guerney, Bernard G., ed. *An Anthology of Russian Literature in the Soviet Period from Gorky to Pasternak.* New York: Vintage, 1960. 452 pages.

Hamalian, Leo, and Arthur Zeigler, eds. *In the Modern Idiom: An Introduction to Literature.* New York: Crowell, 1973. 508 pages.

Hancock, Sheila, and Edward L. Hancock, eds. *Connections: Ideas for Writing.* New York: Harcourt Brace Jovanovich, 1974. 288 pages.

Hardison, O. B., Jr., and Jerry Leath Mills, eds. *The Forms of Imagination: An Anthology of Poetry, Fiction, and Drama.* Englewood Cliffs, New Jersey: Prentice-Hall, 1972. 615 pages.

Hayden, Robert, David J. Burrows, and Frederick R. Lapides, eds. *Afro-American Literature: An Introduction.* New York: Harcourt Brace Jovanovich, 1973. 309 pages.

Hayford, Harrison, and Howard Vincent, eds. *Reader and Writer.* Boston: Houghton Mifflin, 1969. 562 pages.

Hemley, Elaine Gottlieb, and Jack Matthews, eds. *The Writer's Signature: Idea in Story and Essay.* Glenview, Illinois: Scott, Foresman, 1972. 222 pages.

Herr, Dan, and Joel Wells, eds. *Bodies and Spirits.* Garden City, New York: Doubleday, 1964. 192 pages.

—, eds. *Moments of Truth.* Garden City, New York: Doubleday, 1966. 236 pages.

Hill, Herbert, ed. *Anger and Beyond.* New York: Harper and Row, 1966. 227 pages.

Hollis, James R., ed. *Modern Life Styles.* Glenview, Illinois: Scott, Foresman, 1971. 290 pages.

Holsinger, Rosemary, Camille Jordan, and Leon Levenson, eds. *The Creative Encounter.* Glenview, Illinois: Scott, Foresman, 1971. 373 pages.

Howard, C. Jeriel, and Richard F. Tracz, eds. *The Responsible Man: Essays, Short Stories, Poems.* San Francisco: Canfield, 1972.

Hurtik, Emil. *Insight: A Rhetoric Reader.* Philadelphia: Lippincott, 1970. 480 pages.

Hutchinson, Helene D., ed. *Mixed Bag: Artifacts from the Contemporary Culture.* Glenview, Illinois: Scott, Foresman, 1970. 322 pages.

Johnson, Willoughby, and Thomas M. Davis, eds. *College Reading and College Writing,* revised edition. Glenview, Illinois: Scott, Foresman, 1971. 550 pages.

Jones, Le Roi, ed. *The Moderns.* New York: Corinth Books, 1963. 351 pages.

Jorgensen, Paul A., and Frederick B. Shroyer, eds. *A College Treasury: Prose, Fiction, Drama, Poetry.* New York: Scribner's, 1967. 604 pages.

Kearns, Francis E., ed. *The Black Experience: An Anthology of American Literature from the 1970's.* New York: Viking, 1970. 650 pages.

—, ed. *Black Identity: A Thematic Reader.* New York: Holt, Rinehart and Winston, 1970. 359 pages.

Kinney, Arthur F., Kenneth W. Kuiper, Lynn Z. Bloom, eds. *Symposium.* Boston: Houghton Mifflin, 1969. 1129 pages.

Knoll, Robert E., ed. *Contrasts.* New York: Harcourt, Brace, 1959. 627 pages.

Knott, John R., and Christopher R. Reaske, eds. *Mirrors: An Introduction to Literature.* San Francisco: Canfield, 1972. 508 pages.

Knott, Kenneth S., ed. *Pursuing the American Dream.* Englewood Cliffs, New Jersey: Prentice-Hall, 1976. 336 pages.

Kulik, William R., and Glen A. Omans, eds. *Faces of Authority.* Glenview, Illinois: Scott, Foresman, 1972. 262 pages.

La Valley, Albert J., ed. *The New Consciousness: An Anthology of the New Literature.* Englewood Cliffs, New Jersey: Prentice-Hall, 1972. 567 pages.

Levine, Philip, and Henri Coutelle, eds. *Character and Crisis: A Contemporary Reader.* New York: McGraw-Hill, 1966. 482 pages.

Locke, Louis, William M. Gibson, and George Arms, eds. *An Introduction to Literature.* New York: Holt, Rinehart and Winston, 1967. 2 vols.

Low, David M. *et al,* eds. *A Century of Writers: 1855-1955,* with introduction by Oliver Warner. London: Chatto and Windus, 1955. 736 pages.

McCuen, Joray, and Anthony C. Winkler, eds. *Readings for Writers.* New York: Harcourt Brace Jovanovich, 1974. 512 pages.

McElderry, Bruce R., Jr., ed. *The Realistic Movement in American Writing.* New York: Odyssey Press, 1965. 678 pages.

McNamee, Maurice B., James ʾE. Cronin, and Joseph A. Rogen, eds. *Literary Types and Themes,* 2nd ed. New York: Holt, Rinehart and Winston, 1971. 773 pages.

McNamee, Maurice B., ed. *Reading for Understanding,* 3rd ed. New York: Holt, Rinehart and Winston, 1968. 787 pages.

Madden, David, ed. *American Dreams, American Nightmares.* Carbondale: Southern Illinois University Press, 1970. 229 pages.

Mahoney, John, and John Schmittroth, eds. *New Fiction, Non-Fiction.* Englewood Cliffs, New Jersey: Prentice-Hall, 1971. 255 pages.

Margolies, Edward, ed. *A Native Sons Reader.* Philadelphia: Lippincott, 1970. 361 pages.

Michener, James A., ed. *Firstfruits: A Harvest of 25 Years of Israeli Writing.* Philadelphia: Jewish Publishing Society of America, 1973. 344 pages.

Minot, Stephen, ed. *Three Genres: The Writing of Poetry, Fiction, and Drama.* Englewood Cliffs, New Jersey: Prentice-Hall, 1971. 395 pages.

Montague, Gene, Marjorie Henshaw, and Nicolas Salerno, eds. *The Experience of Literature,* 2nd ed. Englewood Cliffs, New Jersey: Prentice-Hall, 1970. 803 pages.

Morgan, Fred, ed. *Here and Now: An Approach to Writing Through Perception.* New York: Harcourt Brace Jovanovich, 1968. 228 pages.

—, ed. *Here and Now II: An Approach to Writing Through Perception.* New York: Harcourt Brace Jovanovich, 1972. 225 pages.

Morris, Alton C., Biron Walker, Philip Bradshaw, John C. Hodges, and Mary E. Whitten, eds. *College English: The First Year,* Sixth Edition. New York: Harcourt Brace Jovanovich, 1973. 878 pages.

Morris, Alton C., Biron Walker, and Philip Bradshaw, eds. *Imaginative Literature: Fiction, Drama, Poetry,* 2nd ed. New York: Harcourt Brace Jovanovich, 1973. 329 pages.

Muscatine, Charles, and Marlene Griffith, eds. *The American Vision: Individual and Collective Voices.* Glenview, Illinois: Scott, Foresman, 1973. 400 pages.

Ohlsen, Woodrow, and Frank Hammond, eds. *Frames of References: An Introduction to Literature.* Belmont, California: Wadsworth, 1974. 399 pages.

Orlovitz, Gil, ed. *The Award Avant-Garde Reader.* New York: Award Books, 1965. 254 pages.

Pearson, Carol, and Katherine Pope, eds. *Who Am I This Time?: Female Portraits in British and American Literature.* New York: McGraw-Hill, 1976. 288 pages.

Perrine, Laurence, ed. *Literature: Structure, Sound, and Sense,* 2nd ed. New York: Harcourt Brace Jovanovich, 1974. 1508 pages.

Pickering, James H., and E. Fred Carlisle, eds. *The Harper Reader.* New York: Harper and Row, 1971. 530 pages.

Radner, Sanford R., and Susan G., eds. *Language and Literature for Composition.* New York: Crowell, 1973. 569 pages.

Rall, Eilene M., and Karl E. Snyder, eds. *Structures in Composition.* Glenview, Illinois: Scott, Foresman, 1970. 522 pages.

Reaske, Christopher R., ed. *The College Writer's Guide to the Study of Literature.* New York: Random House, 1970. 191 pages.

Richardson, H. Edward, ed. *How to Think and Write.* Glenview, Illinois: Scott, Foresman, 1971. 476 pages.

Rockas, Leo, ed. *Modes of Rhetoric.* New York: St. Martin's, 1964. 255 pages.

Rosenheim, Edward W., Jr., ed. *What Happens in Literature.* Chicago: University of Chicago Press, 1960. 162 pages.

Sanders, Charles, ed. *The Scope of Satire.* Glenview, Illinois: Scott, Foresman, 1971. 258 pages.

Sanders, Thomas E., and Franklin D. Hester, eds. *The Now Reader.* Glenview, Illinois: Scott, Foresman, 1969. 241 pages.

Sanders, Thomas E., ed. *Speculations: An Introduction to Literature Through Fantasy and Science Fiction.* Beverly Hills, California: Glencoe Press, 1973. 608 pages.

Schorer, Mark, ed. *Galaxy: Literary Modes and Genres.* New York: Harcourt Brace Jovanovich, 1967. 620 pages.

Schorer, Mark, Philip Durham, and Everett L. Jones, eds. *Harbrace College Reader,* 4th ed. New York: Harcourt Brace

Jovanovich, 1974. 608 pages.

Shrodes, Caroline, Harry Finestone, and Michael F. Shugrue, eds. *The Conscious Reader.* New York: Macmillan, 1974. 1037 pages.

Shrodes, Caroline, Clifford Josephson, and James R. Wilson, eds. *Reading for Rhetoric,* 3rd edition. New York: Macmillan, 1975. 624 pages.

Simonson, Harold P., ed. *Quartet: A Book of Stories, Plays, Poems, and Critical Essays.* New York: Harper and Row, 1970. 1019 pages.

—, eds. *Trio: A Book of Stories, Plays, and Poems.* New York: Harper and Row, 1970. 747 pages.

Somer, John and Joseph Cozzo, eds. *Literary Experience: Public and Private Voices.* Glenview, Illinois: Scott, Foresman, 1971. 681 pages.

Stafford, William T., ed. *Twentieth-Century American Writing.* New York: Odyssey, 1965. 712 pages.

Stallman, Robert W., and R. E. Watters, eds. *The Creative Reader.* New York: The Ronald Press, 1954. 923 pages.

Stanley, Linda, and Sheena Gillespie, eds. *The Treehouse: An Introduction to Literature.* Cambridge, Massachusetts: Winthrop Publishers, 1974. 368 pages.

Trilling, Lionel, ed. *The Experience of Literature.* New York: Holt, Rinehart and Winston, 1967. 1320 pages.

Waite, Harlow O., and Benjamin F. Atkinson, eds. *Literature for Our Time.* New York: Holt, Rinehart and Winston, 1958. 1009 pages.

Zeigler, Arthur, and Leo Hamalian, eds. *In the Modern Idiom: An Introduction to Literature.* New York: Crowell, 1973. 528 pages.

V. HISTORY, THEORY, AND CRITICISM
OF THE SHORT STORY

Ahnebrink, Lars. *Beginnngs of Naturalism in American Fiction: A Study of the Works of Hamlin Garland, Stephen Crane, and Frank Norris.* New York: Russell and Russell, Inc., 1961. 503 pages.

Allen, Walter, ed. *Writers on Writing.* New York: The Writer, Inc., 1948. 258 pages.

Altenbernd, Lynn, and Leslie L. Lewis. *A Handbook for the Study of Fiction.* New York: Macmillan, 1966. 84 pages.

Antico, John, and Meredith K. Hazelrigg. *Insight Through Fiction: Dealing Effectively with the Short Story.* Menlo Park, California: Cummings, 1970. 466 pages.

Beach, Joseph Warren. *American Fiction 1920-1940.* New York: Macmillan, 1941. 371 pages.

Beachcroft, T. D., ed. *The English Short Story.* London: Longmans, Green, 1964. 2 vols.

—. *The Modest Art: A Survey of the Short Story in English.* London and New York: Oxford University Press, 1968. 286 pages.

Block, Haskell M. *Naturalistic Triptych: The Fictive and the Real in Zola, Mann, and Dreiser.* New York: Random House, 1970. 114 pages.

Bone, Robert A. *The Negro Novel in America.* New Haven, Connecticut: Yale University Press, 1958. 268 pages.

Booth, Wayne C. *The Rhetoric of Fiction.* Chicago: University of Chicago Press, 1961. 455 pages.

Borges, Jorge Luis, and others, eds. *Borges on Writing.* New York: E. P. Dutton, 1973. 173 pages.

Boulton, Marjorie. *The Anatomy of Prose.* London: Routledge and Kegan Paul, 1968. 190 pages.

Canby, Henry Seidel. *The Short Story in English.* New York: Henry Holt and Company, 1909. 365 pages.

Cather, Willa. *Willa Cather on Writing,* ed. Stephen Tennant. New York: A. A. Knopt, 1949. 126 pages.

Chekhov, Anton. *Anton Chekhov's Letters on the Short Story, the Drama, and Other Literary Topics,* ed. Louis S. Friedland. New York: Putnam, 1924. 346 pages.

Conrad, Joseph. *Joseph Conrad on Fiction,* ed. Walter F. Wright. Lincoln: University of Nebraska Press, 1973.

Cooke, Michael, ed. *Modern Black Novelists: A Collection of Critical Essays.* Englewood Cliffs, New Jersey: Prentice-Hall, 1971. 219 pages.

Farrell, James T. *A Note on Literary Criticism.* New York: Vanguard, 1936. 221 pages.

Fogle, Richard Harter, ed. *The Romantic Movement in American Writing.* New York: Odyssey Press, 1966. 664 pages.

Forster, E. M. *Aspects of the Novel.* New York: Harcourt, Brace and Company, 1927. 250 pages.

Foulke, Robert, and Paul Smith, eds. *An Anatomy of Literature.* New York: Harcourt Brace Jovanovich, 1972. 1125 pages.

Friederich, Werner P. *History of German Literature.* New York: Barnes and Noble, 1961. 356 pages.

Galloway, David D. *The Absurd Hero in American Fiction.* Austin: University of Texas Press, 1966. 257 pages.

Garland, Hamlin. *Crumbling Idols: Twelve Essays on Art Dealing Chiefly with Literature, Painting, and the Drama.* Chicago and Cambridge, Massachusetts: Stone and Kimball, 1894. 192 pages.

Gordon, Caroline. *How to Read a Novel.* New York: Viking Press, 1957. 247 pages.

Gordon, Edward J. *Writing about Imaginative Literature.* New York: Harcourt Brace Jovanovich, 1973. 196 pages.

Guerin, Wilfred L. *A Handbook of Critical Approaches to Literature.* New York: Harper and Row, 1966. 238 pages.

Guttmann, Allen. *The Jewish Writer in America: Assimiliation and the Crisis of Identity.* New York: Oxford University Press, 1971. 256 pages.

Hale, Nancy. *The Realities of Fiction.* Boston: Little, Brown, 1962. 247 pages.

Hamilton, Clayton. *The Art of Fiction.* New York: The Odyssey Press, 1939. 326 pages.

Hauck, Richard B. *A Cheerful Nihilism: Confidence and "The Absurd" in American Humorous Fiction.* Bloomington: Indiana University Press, 1971. 269 pages.

Hauk, Annelle S., and Carlotta L. Bogart. *Understanding the Short Story.* New York: Odyssey Press, 1969.

Hoffman, Daniel G. *Form and Fable in American Fiction.* New York: Oxford University Press, 1965, c1961. 368 pages.

Ingram, Forrest L. *Representative Short Story Cycles of the Twentieth Century: Studies in a Literary Genre.* The Hague: Mouton, 1971. 234 pages.

James, Henry. *The Art of Fiction and Other Essays,* with introduction by Morris Roberts. New York: Oxford University Press, 1948. 240 pages.

—. *The Art of the Novel,* with introduction by R. P. Blackmur.

New York: Scribner's, 1934. 348 pages.

James, Henry. *The Notebooks of Henry James,* ed. F. O. Matthiessen and Kenneth B. Murdock. New York and London: Oxford University Press, 1947. 425 pages.

—. *Theory of Fiction,* ed. James E. Miller, Jr. Lincoln: University of Nebraska Press, 1972. 366 pages.

Joyce, James. *The Critical Writings of James Joyce.* New York: Viking, 1974. 288 pages.

Kaplan, Harold. *The Passive Voice: An Approach to Modern Fiction.* Athens, Ohio: Ohio University Press, 1973. 239 pages.

Kazin, Alfred. *On Native Grounds: An Interpretation of Modern American Prose Literature.* Garden City, New York: Doubleday, 1956. 425 pages.

Kermode, John Frank. *The Sense of an Ending: Studies in the Theory of Fiction.* New York: Oxford University Press, 1967. 187 pages.

Knott, William C. *The Craft of Fiction.* Englewood Cliffs, New Jersey: Prentice-Hall, 1973. 152 pages.

Lesser, Simon O. *Fiction and the Unconscious.* Boston: Beacon Press, 1957. 322 pages.

Lieberman, Elias. *The American Short Story: A Study of the Influence of Locality in Its Development.* Ridgewood, New Jersey: The Editor, 1912. 203 pages.

Lubbock, Percy. *The Craft of Fiction,* with preface by Mark Schorer. New York: Viking, 1957. 274 pages.

Martin, Jay. *Harvests of Change: American Literature, 1865-1914.* Englewood Cliffs, New Jersey: Prentice-Hall, 1967. 382 pages.

Matthews, Brander. *The Short Story.* New York: American Book Company, 1907. 307 pages.

Matthiessen, F. O. *American Renaissance.* New York: Oxford University Press, 1941. 678 pages.

Miller, James E., Jr., ed. *Myth and Method: Modern Theories of Fiction.* Lincoln: University of Nebraska Press, 1973. 165 pages.

Morse, Donald. *The Choices of Fiction.* Cambridge, Massachusetts: Winthrop Publishers, 1974. 375 pages.

Munson, Gorham. *Style and Form in American Prose.* Port Washington, New York: Kennikat Press, 1969, c1929. 313 pages.

O'Brien, Edward J. *The Advance of the American Short Story,* revised edition. New York: Dodd, 1931. 314 pages.

O'Connor, Frank. *The Lonely Voice: A Study of the Short Story.* Cleveland: World, 1963. 220 pages.

O'Connor, William Van. *Seven Modern American Novelists.* New York and Toronto: New American Library, 1968. 280 pages.

O'Faolain, Sean. *The Short Story.* New York: Devin-Adair, 1951. 370 pages.

Pattee, Fred Lewis. *The Development of the American Short Story: An Historical Survey.* New York: Harper and Brothers, 1923. 392 pages.

Pizer, Donald. *Realism and Naturalism in Nineteenth-Century American Literature.* Carbondale: Southern Illinois University Press, 1966. 176 pages.

Poe, Edgar Allan. *Literary Criticism of Edgar Allan Poe,* ed. Robert L. Hough. Lincoln: University of Nebraska Press, 1965. 155 pages.

Ross, Danforth. *The American Short Story.* Minneapolis: University of Minnesota Press, 1961. 48 pages.

Savage, Arthur W., and Norman W. Wilson, eds. *How to Analyze the Short Story.* Boston: Branden Press, 1971. 89 pages.

Scholes, Robert. *Elements of Fiction.* New York: Oxford University Press, 1968. 88 pages.

Sherr, Paul. *The Short Story and the Oral Tradition.* San Francisco: Boyd and Fraser, 1970. 398 pages.

Singleton, Ralph H. *The Art of Prose Fiction.* Cleveland: World Publishing Company, 1967. 109 pages.

Skaggs, Merrill M. *The Folk of Southern Fiction: A Study in Local-Color Tradition.* Athens, Georgia: University of Georgia Press, 1972.

Starke, Catherine J. *Black Portraiture in American Fiction.* New York: Basic Books, 1971. 280 pages.

Sullivan, Walter. *Death By Melancholy: Essays on Modern Southern Fiction.* Baton Rouge: Louisiana State University Press, 1972.

Surmelian, Leon. *Techniques of Fiction Writing: Measure and Madness,* with introduction by Mark Schorer. Garden City, New York: Doubleday, 1968. 255 pages.

Uzzell, Thomas H., and Camelia White Uzzell. *Narrative Technique: A Practical Course in Literary Psychology.* New York: Harcourt, Brace, 1934. 517 pages.

Vickery, John B., and Jonathan M. Sellery, eds. *The Scapegoat: Ritual and Literature.* Boston: Houghton Mifflin, 1972. 386 pages.

Voss, Arthur. *The American Short Story.* Norman: University of Oklahoma Press, 1973. 399 pages.

Walcutt, Charles. *American Literary Naturalism: A Divided Stream.* Minneapolis: University of Minnesota Press, 1956. 332 pages.

—. *Man's Changing Mask: Modes and Methods of Characterization in Fiction.* Minneapolis: University of Minnesota

Press, 1966. 368 pages.

Ward, Alfred C. *Aspects of the Modern Short Story.* Folcroft, Pennsylvania: Folcroft Press, 1969 reprint of 1924 edition. 307 pages.

Wasserstrom, William. *The Genius of American Fiction.* Boston: Allyn and Bacon, 1970. 472 pages.

Welty, Eudora. *Short Stories.* New York: Harcourt, Brace, 1950, c1949. 53 pages.

West, Ray B., Jr. *The Art of Writing Fiction.* New York: Crowell, 1968. 304 pages.

—. *Reading the Short Story.* New York: Crowell, 1968. 239 pages.

—. *The Short Story in America, 1900-1950.* Freeport, New York: Books for Libraries, 1968 reprint of 1952 edition. 147 pages.

Wharton, Edith. *The Writing of Fiction.* New York: Farrar, Straus and Giroux, reprint of 1925 edition. 178 pages.

Williams, Blanche Colton. *Our Short Story Writers.* Freeport, New York: Books for Libraries Press, 1969 reprint of 1922 edition. 384 pages.

Wilson, Edmund. *The wound and the Bow: Seven Studies in Literature.* London and New York: Oxford University Press, 1959, c1941. 295 pages.

Wisse, Ruth R. *The Schlemiel as Modern Hero.* Chicago: University of Chicago Press, 1971. 134 pages.

Young, Philip. *Three Bags Full: Essays in American Fiction.* New York: Harcourt Brace Jovanovich, 1972. 231 pages.